Beadwork Techniques
of the Native Americans

by Scott Sutton

Published by: Crazy Crow Trading Post

P.O. Box 847
Pottsboro, Texas 75076
(903) 786-2287
www.crazycrow.com

Photo: Custer Battlefield Trading Post

Cover Beadwork: by Scott Sutton

Edited by: Barry E. Hardin & Jerry Smith

Designed by: Michael Catellier,   J. Rex Reddick

Graphic Designer & Illustrated by: Michael Catellier

Illustrations by: Scott Sutton, Jerry Smith, Barry E. Hardin

Photographs by: Scott Sutton, Michael Catellier,
Ginger and Rex Reddick,   Barry E. Hardin,
Andy Russell,   Custer Battlefield Trading Post

ISBN 1-929572-11-5

Editor's Note:

Projects such as this book are but stepping stones upon which the next researchers can build. As such, this work by Scott Sutton is the culmination of much learning on his part, from the teachings of others as well as the fruits of his own experience. Presented here are the results of his many years of dedicated work. However, this book, like most projects, would not have been possible without the assistance of others. We especially wish to thank the following for their gracious contributions: Custer Battlefield Trading Post, Mike Catellier, Don Drefke, Richard Greene, Keven Hiebert, Adam Lovell, Jerry Smith, Rex and Ginger Reddick, Mike Tucker, Museum of the Great Plains, Morning Star Gallery and, finally, the many Native American artisans who have gone on but left us this rich legacy of craftwork which we endeavor to respectfully follow.

Content

Beadwork Techniques
of the Native Americans

Macaw Fan: by Mike Tucker & Steve Smith

Reddick Collection

Introduction

After viewing hundreds of examples of Native American beadwork, there are certain qualities that give each work that classic "Indian Look": Colors, designs, scale and layouts are some of these qualities. Most important are the style and the technique in which the beadwork is done. This book is a "HOW TO" book covering four styles of beadwork: loom, two needle appliqué, peyote or gourd stitch, and, finally, lazy stitch. The technique for each style is presented in great detail. The numerous photos and the up close illustrations are an integral part of these details. My goal is to present enough information in a clear and understandable form so that starting your own beadwork project will be as trouble free as possible. These techniques are used in beading items for the dance clothes and street wear of both men and women. Using my methods, coupled with diligent research on your part, you should soon be able to do quality beadwork with that "Indian Look".

Crow Cradle:
Photo by Custer Battlefield Trading Post

Supplies 1

Quality of Supplies:

Having the correct beads, threads, needles and beeswax is extremely important. Any craftsman knows that the quality of the supplies used makes the difference between a project that will hold up for years and one that may fall apart. There are many traders throughout the country that have quality supplies. Most can be found on the internet. Talk to craftspeople in your locale that have been doing beadwork for some time and get opinions as to where they get their quality supplies.

Beads:

Beads have a long history of importance in establishing trade relations with, not only American Indians, but the native peoples throughout the world. Throughout time, beads have been used as trade items, for adornment, and to create works of art. Today, the beads used by Native Americans who create masterful and artful beadwork come from several places. The Czech Republic, Japan, Germany, France and Italy all make beads. (See: *The History of Beads Concise Edition by* Dubin.)

There are several styles of beads. "Seed beads" are the most common beads currently used in Native American beadwork. Other types of beads used are bugle, "cuts" or charlottes, iris, tri-cut, delicas and white hearts. Some other types that may be used to help complete a project might be pony beads, crow beads, fire polish, or crystal beads. Since this book deals with four styles of beadwork which predominately use seed beads, a more detailed description of these is warranted. Seed beads are small glass beads, either opaque or transparent, that, depending on origin, have different sizing scales. Czech beads, probably the most common, come in hanks or bunches (or sometimes loose) that are sized such that the larger number indicates a smaller bead. The sizes most commonly used are 13/0 (pronounced "thirteen-ott" or "thirteen oh"), 12/0, and 11/0. Other sizes available include 18/0, 16/0, 15/0, 14/0, 10/0, and 8/0. These are used in some specialty cases that will be mentioned under each style of beadwork. Historically, the Italians used a different number system for seed beads which included 4/0 and 5/0.

For a given project, there is no fast rule as to which seed beads to use. Some are more readily available, others have bigger holes, some are more uniform in size, and still others are special shades of color that only come from one region. Regardless of which beads you choose for your project, there are some things that must be considered. For example, an Italian 4/0 is similar to a Czech 12/0, but not exactly; so, they may not work well in the same project. However, because of a certain desired color or special effect, beads may have to be mixed. Indians have been doing this for a long time.

In earlier times, of course, seed beads were not as widely available as they are today, nor were they as uniformly manufactured. Consequently, an Indian beadworker would have to take what she could get. This often meant that her seed bead collection reflected a variety of sizes, in order to also contain the several colors that she commonly used. But, being ever adaptable, she quickly learned how to integrate beads of different sizes into the same project. Examples of this are most widely seen in appliqué work. Also, examinations of Plains lazy stitch work of the 1800s will often reveal the use of 2 or 3 different seed bead sizes on the same pipebag or dress, for example. **(Ex. 1.01)**

Ex. 1.01 Cheyenne moccasin exhibiting the use of mixed bead sizes, presumably to obtained the colors desired by the artist. Reddick Collection.

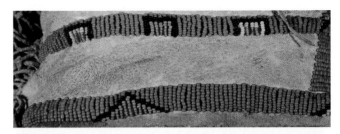

It is strongly recommend that you purchase enough beads to finish the project or group of projects if making a set of beadwork. Beads, like any dyed item, may vary from batch to batch. There is nothing more disappointing than starting a big project, running out of a background color, and not being able to match that color again. Slight changes in background color may be very noticeable. (**Ex. 1.02**)

Ex. 1.02 Sioux Woman's Dress. Don Drefke Collection

The proper use of colors is very important to the success of a design or project. In doing Native American beadwork, particularly a period piece (one from a specific time such as the late 1800s), some research is warranted. It is beyond the scope of this book to go into details on designs. There is so much tribal variation in designs, as well as historic pieces versus contemporary pieces, that the techniques (the focus of this book) would get lost in the explanation. However, a few comments are worth reviewing. Historically, some tribes used certain background colors and design colors, whereas contemporary pieces may use just about any color. Even though background colors may vary greatly, the design colors must be in sharp contrast with the background color. The goal should be to avoid colors that blend or meld together. It helps to think two dimensionally: dark on light and light on dark. Even when doing a rainbow effect, use bright colors of red, orange and yellow. Avoid using colors like dark red, bright red and light red all next to each other; they just blend into a red blob when viewed from a distance. In pictograph types of design where shading may be necessary to give dimension to the subject, it is still important that you be able to see the line of demarcation between the two colors. Remember: contrast is the key!

9

Needles:

There are basically 3 types of needles: Sharps, Beading, and Glover's needles. Sharps come in 4 sizes: 10S, 11S, 12S and 13S. Size 10 is larger than size 13. These needles are short and very sharp. They are used for lazy stitch, appliqué, peyote, and edge work. Beading needles come in 10B, 12B, 13B and 16B sizes. These needles are longer and have thinner eyes that sometimes break easily. They are primarily used in loom beading, although some people prefer to use Sharps for all their work. Whether Sharps or Beading needles are used, the size gives reference to the smallest bead the needle will pass through easily. The thickness of the thread has a great deal to do with this as well. The third type of needle is called a Glover's needle. They come in size 4 and 8. Glover's needles are designed for sewing leather pieces together. They have a very sharp point with a triangular tip that is designed to cut the hide as it passes through.

Bead Size	Thread Size				Needle Sizes							
	00	A	B	D	10S	11S	12S	13S	10B	12B	13B	16B
10/0				X	X				X			
11/0			X	X		X				X		
12/0			X				X			X		
13/0	X	X					X				X	
14/0	X	X										X
16/0	X											X

Fig. 1

Needles are manufactured in several countries. The finest quality comes from England. They tend to have stronger eyes than those manufactured in other countries. (No scientific study here, just experience).

I tend to favor short needles for all my work. I use predominantly 11S and 12S needles from England. A word of caution here: Most of these needles can be almost as sharp at the eye end as at the tip. Be careful. Poking yourself with the back end of a needle is not pleasant. Make a leather thimble out of some scrap leather and electrical or first aid tape to protect the finger with which you push the needle. Metal thimbles tend to break the eye of the needle.

Thread:

Several types of thread are used in doing beadwork. Currently, a thread called Nymo is the predominant thread used to do the actual beadwork. This is a nylon thread that is rot resistant. It comes in the following sizes ranging from finest to heaviest: "00" is very fine, followed by "A", "B", "C", "D" and "F", which is the thickest (there is no "E"). When each style of beadwork is discussed, the size of the thread used will be reviewed.

When threading a needle with Nymo, it is best to cut it at an angle. **(Fig. 2)** Once cut, do not wax it, do not smooth it or do anything to it. Immediately put the cut end into the eye of the needle and pull the thread through. If the thread splits, repeat the process. After a few attempts, you'll get the hang of it.

Other types of thread are used. White cotton thread, size 12, is used for warp thread in loom beadwork. Mercerized white cotton (button hole) thread may also be used as a warp thread. Finally, sinew, either genuine or simulated, is used for some projects, such as soling a pair of moccasins. A sheet of genuine sinew is split by working it back and forth by hand to break the fibers apart into small threadlike strands. It is important to use the same thickness of sinew throughout a beadwork project. Simulated sinew is usually split for use, depending on the thickness you desire.

Fig. 2

Beeswax:

I am an absolute believer in the use of beeswax. Waxing will coat the thread, allowing it to glide through the beads easier and will help to weatherproof it. It will also help to prevent the thread from tangling. I wax and re-wax frequently. There are some grades of beeswax that are cut with paraffin; avoid these. Use pure beeswax. It is softer, which allows it to cling to the thread better.

When waxing the thread, hold the threaded needle by the eye and pull the thread over the top of the cake of beeswax. As you pull with one hand, you can hold and guide the thread under your other thumb while holding the beeswax cake with that thumb and a couple of fingers. As mentioned above, re-wax frequently, but that does not mean to make the thread "gummy". A gummy thread will only clog the bead and attract dirt to cling to it. Hence, wax often, but not heavily. There is no need to wax genuine sinew.

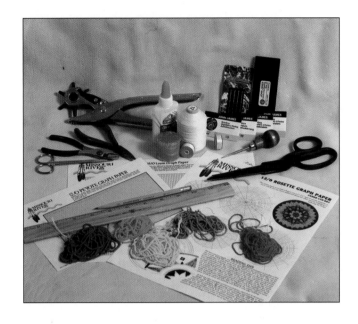

Oklahoma Fans. Reddick Collection

Other Supplies:

Having the right beads, threads, needles and beeswax is important to quality work, but we cannot forget the basics. Good scissors, like those made by the Gingher Company, are essential. I use two different types: the 8 inch bent trimmer, and 4 inch craft scissors. Both may be obtained at a good fabric store or through a quality trader.

Another great tool is a quality rotary leather punch. Again, I use two different types, one to make bigger holes and one for fine holes. The larger one will make holes up to 3/16". These are carried by most stores selling leather goods and by trading posts. There is also a punch that makes precise, very small holes up to 1/16 inch. Both of these tools are good to have, but a reminder here is to buy quality items that will last.

Additional tools to have include awls, needle nose pliers, flat blade pliers (to break a bead), embroidery hoops, a loom, a ruler with grid marks, quality bonded paper, and writing instruments (fine point pens and pencils). The sum total of these tools will cost about $150. Having them will make your life as a craftsperson more enjoyable.

One final item is glue. Aleene's Tacky Glue ® is the best for craftwork. This is white glue that dries clear, pliable and water resistant. It may be used on fabric, leather, paper or metal. Although other types of glues could be used, in my experience, this is the best.

Pottawatomi Loom Beaded
Bandolier Bag
Reddick Collection

Loom Beadwork 2

Loom Beaded Belt, Sokagon Ojibway -
Reddick Collection

Loom Beading:

Loom Beadwork is a woven style of beadwork used to create bands or strips. Often the completed strips are sewn to a backing of soft leather, a piece of strap leather, or to cloth. Loom beadwork gets its name from the device, the loom, which is strung with long threads. Beads are woven in between these threads, called "warp threads." The thread upon which the beads are actually strung is called "the weft thread". This style is used a great deal in making belts and other items for men's dance clothes, particularly Grass Dance, Straight Dance, and Fancy Dance outfits.

Loom Beading Materials:

Needles: Beading needles: 10B, 12B, 13B or 16B are used. Some people prefer Sharps in the same sizes.

Thread: Warp threads: Use heavy cotton or buttonhole thread. Weft thread: use Nymo size D.

Beads: Any size may be used. Most common are 11/0 Czech, but 13/0, 12/0, 10/0, 13/0 charlottes (cuts), or 11/0 charlottes (cuts) may be used.

Backing: Leather, any type. Suede cloth, canvas or wool may also be used.

Miscellaneous: Scissors, beeswax, masking/electrical/duct tape

Loom Construction:

Before any loom beadwork can be done, a loom must be acquired or constructed. Basically, a loom consists of a base and two uprights. There are probably as many different ways to make a loom as there are those who do lots of loom beadwork. However, some key points to consider are: strength of the wood, roughness of the wood, length of the longest piece of beadwork to be done, and width of the widest piece of beadwork to be done. Also, the height of the uprights must be tall enough to allow your hands to maneuver under the warp threads. Glue and screws are recommended to fix the uprights to the base instead of using nails. Metal "L" brackets are useful. Making your loom adjustable is a good idea, as your projects will most likely vary in length. Review the photos to get some ideas for constructing your own loom, or purchase an adjustable loom from a reputable trading post.

A sturdy, easy-to-make adjustable bead loom is illustrated below in Figure 1, plus Photos on page 16. The dimensions are suggestions, so you can make yours differently to fit your particular needs. Make from 3/4" wood stock. Materials are available at any major hardware store.

The finished adjustable loom consists of two pieces: a long fixed base with a slot in the middle, and the sliding base. The sliding base has a bolt that fits through it which extends through the slot in the fixed base. The threaded end of the bolt sticks up through the sliding base, and a large wing nut caps the bolt. By loosening the wing nut, the sliding base can be moved up and down the fixed base to whatever position you wish, based on the length of strip you intend to bead. There is an added bonus to this design: Often, no matter how hard you try, some of the warp threads you string up are a little loose. By making an adjustment to the position of the sliding base, it is often possible to tighten up these strings.

We recommend that you use wood screws wherever possible, as nails will tend to loosen and pull out over time. File a slight groove in the tops of the bases to hold the springs in place. Springs should be of fine wire, tightly wound, about 9" total length. The spring should spread slightly as you attach each end to the side screws.

Figure 1 through 6: Adjustable Bead Loom Construction

Fig. 1

Wood Loom: Dimensions

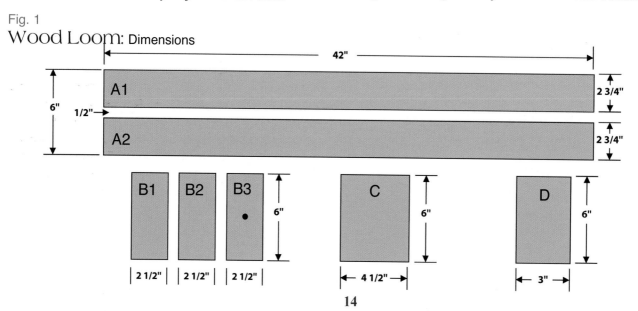

Fig. 2
Spring: A 9" spring is best for this size loom.

Fig. 3
Sliding Base: Side View Adjustable End.

Use wood screws to join pieces
as shown.

Metal "L" Bracket

Wing Nut

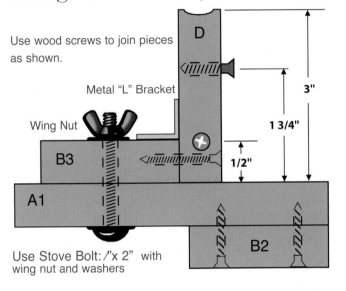

D

3"

1 3/4"

1/2"

B3

A1

Use Stove Bolt: /"x 2" with
wing nut and washers

B2

Bead Loom Hardware List:

(2) 9" springs: approximately 22 coils per inch with a loop on
each end.
(1) Thumb screw: 1/4" - 20 x 2"
(2) Washers: 1/4" hole x 1" diameter
(1) Wing Nut: 1/4" - #20
(10) Phillips Screws: 5/8" - #8
(16) Wood Screws: 1" - #8

Fig. 5
Phillips-Head Wood Screw:
5/8'' - #8

Screw in until all threads are in the wood and only
the collar of the screw is exposed.

5/8'' and 1"

Fig. 4
End Base: Side View

Use wood screws to join pieces
as shown.

Attach spring ends to the
side screws.

C

A2

B1

Fig. 6
End View:

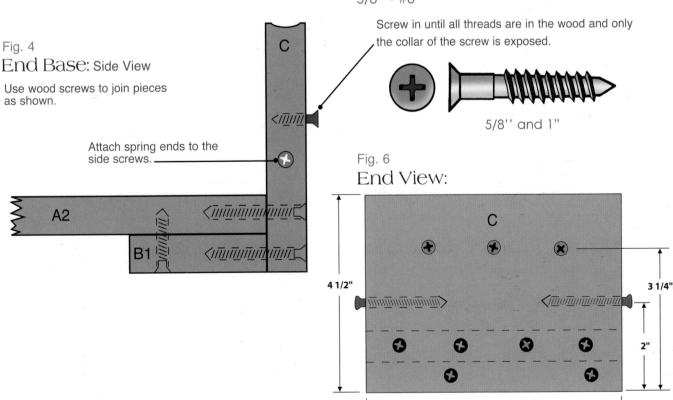

C

4 1/2"

3 1/4"

2"

6"

Loom: Inside View

Loom: End View

Final Adjustable Bead Loom:

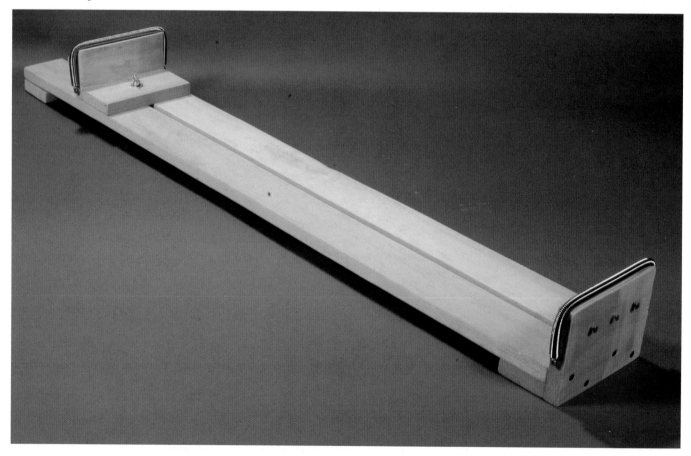

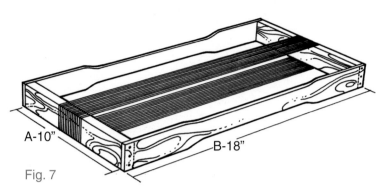

Fig. 7

Constructing a Box Loom:

Another simple, authentic loom is the Box Loom (**Fig. 7**). So-named for obvious reasons, it is non-adjustable. However, it is ideal for beading wide pieces, such as bandolier bag panels, etc. It is constructed from simple materials, such as scraps you might have in your workshop.

See Figure 7. The sides marked "A" are those on which the thread will be wrapped, and these should be the thickest of the 4 sides. (We suggest 3/4" x 2" pine.) The sides marked "B" may be of thinner wood, possibly 1/2" x 2" plywood. The lengths of "A" and "B", as shown, are strictly arbitrary and should be governed by your own needs and the sizes of your projects. We suggest, however, that you not limit yourself by making the box too small to accommodate long or wide bead strips. Sand the edges of sides "A" smooth and rounded to keep them from cutting the threads.

After constructing the frame, string the loom as follows: Estimate how wide the bead strip is to be and divide that measurement in half. Make a light mark at that distance from the center of the loom, then simply wrap the thread once around the loom at that point and tie the thread to itself. Continue to wrap thread around the loom until you have the number of threads needed for your strip, then tie the thread off to itself. (Note: The author recommends using double threads for the outside warp threads.) As you wrap, be sure that the threads are snug enough to not slide on the loom. Also, if snug enough, they should seat themselves into the wood, thus making a natural spacer for each thread as you wrap.

Draw a Design:

Before stringing your loom, the desired design needs to be drawn. It is convenient to use seed bead graph paper (included in this book) to plot out at least a portion of the design. Color in the design with colored pencils so that there is a blue print for each bead row. In this way you will know how many beads of each color to pick up and in what sequence to pick them up. If the design repeats, and most do, you only need to draw out one element.

In picking your design, start with something simple, and then, as you progress, view lots of Indian work on the internet, in books, and in museums to develop your artistic sense. You will find that, though some pieces feature tribal designs, others feature "Pan-Indian" designs. Pan-Indian designs are the sets of designs and common elements used by just about any Native bead worker regardless of his or her tribal affiliation. They reflect regional, rather than tribal, differences. Geometric designs in combination with rainbow color changes, black and white eagle tail feathers, tepees and horses are common Pan–Indian motifs. Most often loom work features geometric designs, though some abstract floral elements are common on some pieces, such as Prairie belts. **(Ex. 2.01: Prairie Belt)**

Ex. 2.01 Prairie Belt, Collected Osage -
Reddick Collection

Stringing the Loom:

Note: Make sure the bead dividers on the loom (springs in the adjustable loom example) have approximately the same spacing as the beads you are using. A string of beads, in the size you are going to use and affixed to the top of the upright, makes a very good divider. A shallow groove across the top of the upright will help stabilize the bead string. Hair combs could be used as dividers.

Ex. 2.02

To string the loom, start in the center and work toward the outside. The strings that span the distance between the uprights of the loom are called warp threads. Though the term "warp threads" is used, there is basically one continuous thread. Use heavy cotton thread for the warp threads, like size 12; do not use Nymo, as nylon is too stretchy. The number of warp strings will equal the number of beads in one row, plus 1. For example, a single row 30 beads wide will require 31 warp threads. **(Fig. 8)**

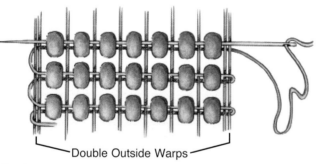

Double Outside Warps

Fig. 8
Illustrations showing one more warp thread than the number of beads (outside warps are doubled).

Use the screw/nail on the back center of the upright and tie the heavy cotton thread to it using a slip knot **(Ex. 2.02)**. I start stringing from the right upright.

The beaded strip demonstrated in **(Ex. 2.02)** through **(Ex. 2.21)** consists of 20 beads and 21 warp threads.

After securing the thread end to the screw, pass the thread through the right dividers and pull across to the left side. **(Ex. 2.03)** Pass the thread through the left dividers exactly opposite the slot on the right divider. Complete the first string by looping around the screw at the center back of the left upright. It is important to continually keep tension on the thread as you string the warp threads.

Ex. 2.03

To string the second thread, bring the thread back up to the left divider, guide the thread into the slot adjacent to the center warp thread and continue to the right divider where you also slot the thread adjacent to the center warp thread. Complete the second thread by looping around the beginning nail/screw. **(Ex. 2.04)** Next, string the third thread on the other side of the center thread and loop around the nail/screw on the back. Continue to string the loom by stringing on both sides of the center warp thread. As you work your way out on wider looms with two or more screws, use the screws closest to the slot occupied by the thread. Continue until the loom is strung as wide as you need it.

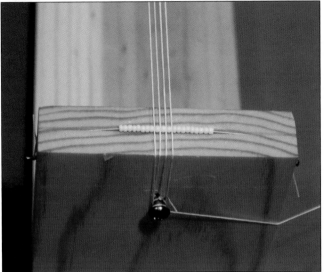

Ex. 2.04

Ex. 2.06

The final outside row, on both sides, may be doubled to add strength to the outside edge. This is not required, but these two extra warp threads will help the loomed piece last longer. Once again, it is important to maintain even tension as the loom is being strung; however, you do not want the warp threads to be extremely tight. Once the end is reached, tie off the thread on one of the nails/screws. **(Ex. 2.05)**

Finally, when the loom is strung, put a piece of duct, electric, or masking tape over the dividers to prevent the threads from jumping out from between the slots. **(Ex. 2.06)**

Once the loom is strung, the beading can begin. To make sure the finished strip will be the correct length, it is best to start in the center of the span of warp threads. **(Ex. 2.07)** Bead until one half of the center design element is complete. The length of this element will allow you to calculate where the remaining elements are to be placed and the amount of background needed between design elements.

Ex. 2.05

Ex. 2.07

Using size D Nymo, thread a long Beading needle. (A Sharps needle can be used if you prefer). Use a single thickness of thread. Do not double it. This thread is called the weft thread. Wax the weft thread moderately and every few rows thereafter. The first row is strategic in the overall appearance of the beaded strip. Following the pattern on the bead graph paper, string the beads on the needle that will make up the center row of the pattern. Pick your beads carefully here. In any hank, there are some very fat beads and some very thin ones; pick only the average size beads. Slide the chosen beads down the weft thread to a point where there are about 12-16 inches of thread left at the end (hereafter referred to as tail string). **(Ex. 2.08)** In my technique, I do not tie the weft to the outside warps but leave it loose for now. Now proceed according to the following photos and instructions: Place the thread with the beads on it under the warp threads. **(Ex. 2.09)**

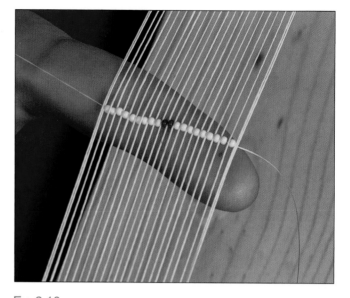

Ex. 2.10

Starting with the beads closest to the needle, push the beads up through the warp threads with your left index finger. **(Ex. 2.10)**

While supporting the beads with the left finger and holding the needle in the right hand, negotiate the needle back through all the beads, making sure the needle is over the top of the warp threads. You can tell if the needle is over the top by seeing the silver glint of the needle over the white of the warp threads. **(Ex. 2.11)**

Ex. 2.08

Ex. 2.11

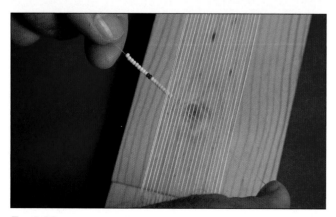

Ex. 2.09

Ex. 2.11a

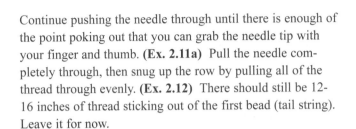

Continue pushing the needle through until there is enough of the point poking out that you can grab the needle tip with your finger and thumb. **(Ex. 2.11a)** Pull the needle completely through, then snug up the row by pulling all of the thread through evenly. **(Ex. 2.12)** There should still be 12-16 inches of thread sticking out of the first bead (tail string). Leave it for now.

Now go through the second row of beads with the needle, and, as with the first, make sure the needle is on top of the warp threads. **(Ex. 2.13a)** Pull the thread through until it is snug, but not overly tight. Repeat this process for a few more rows. **(Fig. 9 & Ex. 2.14)**

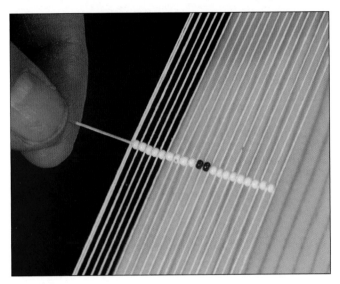

Ex. 2.12

Ex. 2.13a

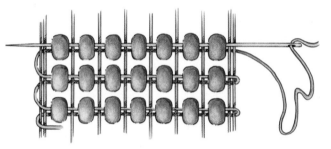

Fig. 9 Details of threads and needle placement.

Avoid pulling so tight that it pulls the right outside warp threads into the end bead. Select and string on the beads for the second row. Go under the warp threads. **(Ex. 2.13)**

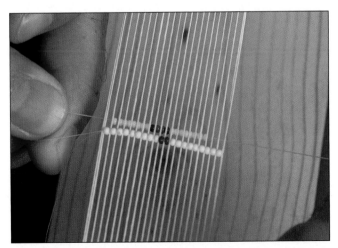

Ex. 2.13

Ex. 2.14

Push the beads up through the warp threads starting with the beads furthest away from the needle. This is opposite of what was done for the first row, but it is what you will do for all the remaining rows.

21

As each new row is put on, it is very important to maintain a uniform row width so that the finished product will not have undulating edges. Uniformity is achieved by very careful bead selection. Different colors in the same size beads may vary slightly in width. Heavy cotton warp threads help ever so slightly with uniformity as the threads act like cushions that allow one row to be snugged up just slightly tighter than another.

Once a few rows are done, it is time to go back and tie off the tail string. Gently pull on the tail string to make sure that the first row is snug but not overly tight. Thread the tail string into a second needle and weave it through the first four beads of the first row, going on top of the warp threads. This is referred to as back-weaving. Bring the needle out on the side of the work facing you between the fourth and fifth bead. **(Ex. 2.15)**

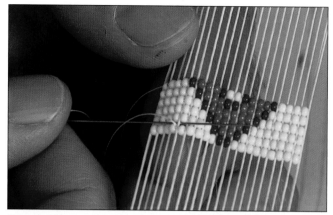

(Ex. 2.16)

(Ex. 2.17)

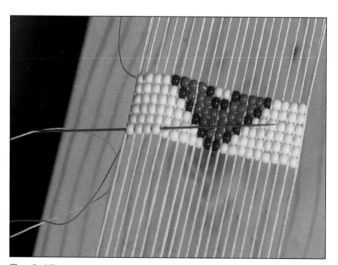

Ex. 2.15

(Ex. 2.18)

Pull the needle through, snug up the thread like any other row, then guide the needle under the warp thread between beads #4 and #5. **(Ex. 2.16)** Come out on the other side of the warp and continue to pull the needle until there is roughly an equal amount of tail string on either side of the warp thread. **(Ex. 2.17)** Remove the needle, pinch the thread on the left side in the middle, then use it to tie a square knot with the piece of thread that had the needle. **(Ex. 2.18)** Clip the threads short, but not too close to the knot. **(Ex. 2.19)** This will be the back of the finished piece, so this knot will never show. All other knots will be tied on this side as well. If you were to tie off the weft at the outside edge (on the double warps), those knots would be seen on the finished piece.

(Ex. 2.19)

When you clip off the excess thread, do not cut too close to the knot. Nymo, being nylon and somewhat stretchy, does have a tendency to loosen up; so, cutting the ends too close to the knot may allow the knot to slip undone.

Continue beading until the thread becomes too short to continue. Remember to re-wax after every couple of rows, enough to coat the thread but not so much that it clogs up the beads. Tie off the thread in the same way as with the tail above, as follows: Go to the left end of the next to the last row you beaded. There, run the needle through the tops of the first 4 beads and tie the thread off around the warp thread between beads #4 and #5 using the square knot method used with the tail string. Clip the threads next to the knot. Start the new thread by going to the right end of the last row beaded. **(Ex. 2.20)** Tie the new weft thread to the warp thread 4-6 beads in using an overhand knot. Pass the needle through the remaining beads to the left of the knot you just tied, exiting at the left side. **(Fig. 10) (Ex. 2.21)**

Ex. 2.20

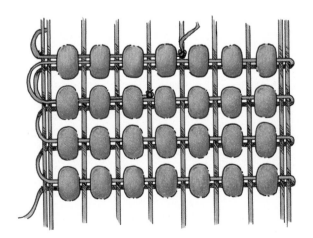

Fig. 10

Ex. 2.21

Continue beading as before until half of the center design is finished. **(Ex. 2.21)**

To bead the other half of the center design, it may be easier to turn the loom around so that you are able to use the same hand to work the needle through. If you are able to work with both hands equally well, this will not be an issue. I turn my loom.

When the beading of the second half of the center design is complete, stop. Measure the complete center pattern. Since you have decided on a length for the finished strip, you will now know how many patterns fit into that length. Let's say there will be 5 repeated patterns including the completed center pattern. So, multiply the length of the center pattern by 5; this is the length needed for the 5 patterns. Knowing the length of the final piece and the total length of the 5 patterns, subtract them. Your answer is the total amount of background inches needed. Divide the background inches by one more than the number of patterns: 6 in this example. The resulting number will be the number of inches of background needed between each pattern and at both ends.

Continue working until the strip is complete. Leave enough weft thread when doing the last rows to be able to back-weave at least three rows. Back-weaving through these rows will strengthen the ends of the beaded strip. After back-weaving three rows or so, tie the thread off as described earlier. Once the thread is tied off, wrap the warp threads at each end with ½" masking tape approximately 1/8" from the end of the work. Pull the edges in a little so that when the taped end is folded under the loomed work, the tape edge will not be seen when mounted. Do this before cutting the warp threads to free the beadwork from the loom. Cutting the beadwork off the loom is a joyous occasion!

Tabs:

If you are making a pair of suspenders and you want to have more of a decorative end, you may want to finish the ends in a set of "tabs" like those pictured.

(Ex. 2.22) Tabs are independently loomed finger-like extensions at the end of the loomed piece. They utilize the warp threads of the main piece. Tabs are generally about 5 to 9 beads wide and may be about 2 inches long if they are on suspenders, 7– 9 inches long if they are part of a pair of garters, and even longer for streamers. This is how you determine the width of each tab:

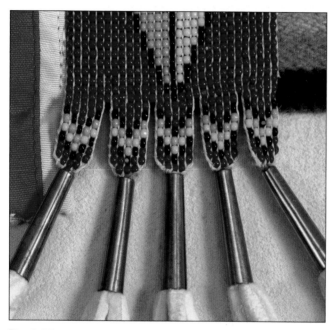

Ex. 2.22

Example 1: Let us say that your loomed piece is 29 beads wide and you want to have a set of 5 tabs. This is how you determine the width of each tab: Subtract 4 from 29, as there will be a missing bead in between each "finger". Divide this result, 25, by 5 (tabs) to get an answer of 5 (beads). In this example, each tab will be 5 beads wide. **(Ex. 2.22)**

Example 2: Let's say this time your loomed piece is 53 beads wide and you want 6 tabs. Subtract 5 from 53 and divide by 6. The result is 8. Each tab will be 8 beads wide.

Example 3: Suppose this time your loomed strip is to be 61 beads wide, and you want 7 tabs. Subtract 6 and divide by 7. Whoa, the answer does not come out even. This means that 7 tabs will not work. Four tabs will not work either, and neither will 3, 5 or 6. Better plan ahead if you want tabs. Plan for tabs when you first draw your pattern.

Detail of Belt, Osage - Jerry Smith Collection

In our next example, we will have 3 tabs on a 29 bead-wide strip. Each tab will be 9 beads wide. When you have reached the point in the loom work where the tabs start, just continue beading with your weft thread. **(Ex. 2.23)** Since the tab is 9 beads wide, bead the rows of the initial tab using the first 10 warp threads until you get to the place where the tab tapers. Usually, the end of each tab is tapered down to a single bead. To start the taper, put 7 beads on the needle, bring them up under all of the warp threads, but only push them up between the 2nd through the 9th warp threads.

(Ex. 2.24) Be sure the weft thread wraps around the 1st and 10th warp threads making them "extra outside warp threads." The next row will have 5 beads, and again 2 extra outside warp threads will be pulled in. **(Fig. 2.35)** Complete the tab by putting on one bead, and there will be 5 warp threads on each side. **(Ex. 2.26)** Tie off the weft thread by wrapping it around all the warp threads and tie a knot. **(Ex. 2.27)**

Ex. 2.23

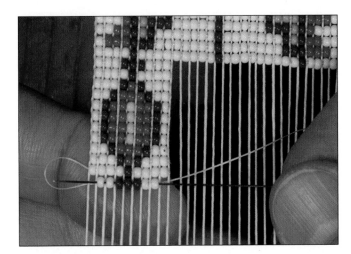

Ex. 2.24

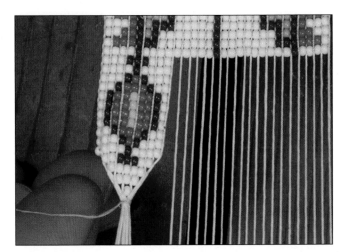

Ex. 2.27

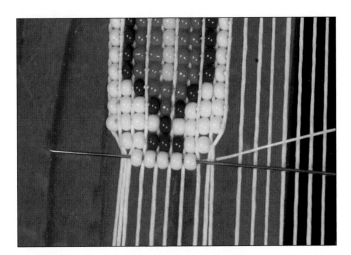

Ex. 2.25

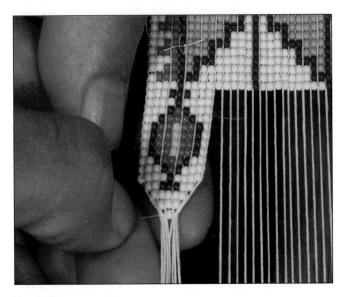

Ex. 2.26

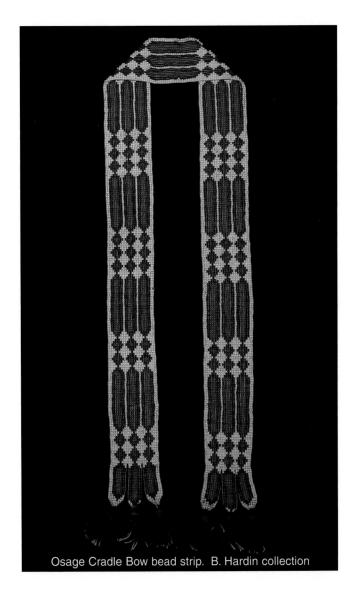

Osage Cradle Bow bead strip. B. Hardin collection

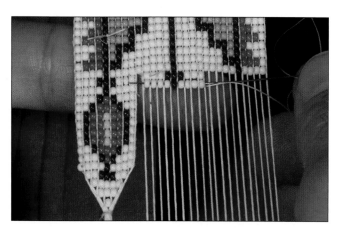

Ex. 2.28

Ex. 2.31

Bead the second tab using weft threads 11 through 20. Start your weft thread for this tab as you would any new thread utilizing the last complete row of 29 beads. **(Ex. 2.28)** Complete this tab just like the first. **(Ex. 2.29)** Once the remaining tab has been beaded and tied off, the suspender can be cut from the loom, but you may want to leave several inches of loose warp threads. Use these loose ends from each tab to tie on dangles. **(Ex. 2.30)** Dangle decorations can be yarn tassels, shells (such as drilled cowries), or coins with drilled holes. **(Ex. 2.31 & 2.32)**

Ex. 2.29

Ex. 2.30

Ex. 2.32

You can also make a beaded loop with each loose warp thread and create a small bunch of bead loops at the tip of each tab. To do so, extra long left-over warp threads are required, as a needle has to be threaded onto each thread to string the beads. Again it is necessary to plan ahead.

Mounting the Bead Strip:

After a bead strip is completed, it should be backed or mounted on leather or some type of heavyweight material. (Ex. 2.33) Some exceptions are garters, streamers and strips for otter drags. If using a soft backing, it is easier to have the backing a little wider than the width of the strip. Once sewn down, the excess is trimmed away. The strip can either be hand sewn or machine stitched.

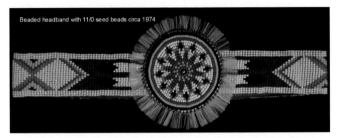

Ex. 2.33 Loom Beaded Headband by Scott Sutton

CAUTION: If sewing on a machine, stitch between the 2nd and 3rd beads in from the side of the strip. It is better to go faster than slow. If sewn too slowly, the needle may strike a bead, causing it or the needle to break. When going fast, the needle seems to glance off the beads.

If the piece is to be mounted on heavy leather, it should be hand sewn. When hand sewing, the key is to make the stitches snug but not overly tight. Overly tight stitching will cause the work to pucker.

Let's talk about mounting a belt. Belt strips are often mounted on strap leather. The strap leather needs to be cut to the desired size before mounting the beadwork. It should also be pre-punched with an awl, as it is too thick to be pierced with a Glover's needle. As a substitute for an awl, a good sewing machine with a heavy-duty needle (but no thread) can be used to pre-punch holes. An alternative is to have the local shoe repairman punch holes with his heavy-duty machine (without thread) following lines you draw.

Careful measurements must be taken to know where to draw the guidelines for punching holes. The stitches should be 4 to 5 beads in from each edge. On the ends, two sets of vertical holes, rather than one, are recommended. These vertical holes should be spaced to sew between the last and next to last row and between rows #6 and #7.

Tack the beaded strip to the strap leather in 6 places using the pre-punched holes, starting first on both sides at the center. Curve the strap leather around as if it were being worn before tacking the top and bottom of each end. It is highly recommended that you sew the loom-beaded strip to the leather belt while it is in this curved position. Sew on the beaded strip with Nymo thread #7. Cotton thread will rot and break over the years, as dancers tend to get the inside of the belt sweaty. Make the stitches snug, but not so tight that the beadwork appears puckered.

CAUTION: *If the beadwork is sewn lying flat, there will be a great deal of stress placed on the mounting stitches when the belt is curved around your waist. This is because the thickness of the strap leather will force the beadwork to occupy a greater circumference. This stress is not good for the future security of the stitches and, ultimately, the beadwork may be pulled out of shape, distorting parts of the design.*

Often when mounted on strap leather, the beadwork is accented with a row of nickel (silver color) or brass spots on either side of the beaded strip. This sets off the work and gives a nice touch to the finished belt. If spots are being used, you must allow for them when planning the width of the strap leather for the beaded belt. A good rule of measurement here is to allow for double the width of the spot on each edge. If you are using a ½-inch spot, you will need to add on an inch; so, the final width of the strap leather will be the width of the beadwork plus one inch. Space the spots about one spot width apart. **(Ex. 2.34)**

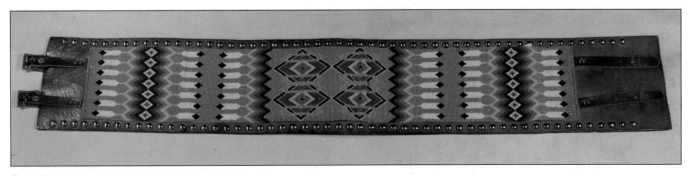

Ex. 2.34 Loom Beaded Belt by Rex Reddick

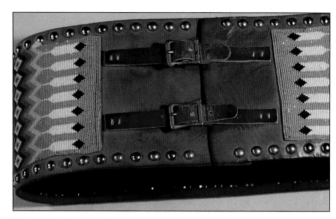

Ex. 2.35 Back of belt showing method of attaching buckles. Rex Reddick

Once the loom work is sewn down and spots added, rivet or sew leather straps and buckles to the ends so the belt can be secured about the waist. **(Ex. 2.35)** Ideally, the leather is long enough so that the ends overlap when being worn. However, the length of the belt seems to "shrink as the dancer gets older" (so to speak), and some even need to add leather extensions and/or longer straps if they want to continue to wear the belt. Leather ties are a reasonable substitute for buckles.

Loomed Belt by Adam Lovell

Loomed Belt by Scott Sutton

Loomed Belt by Scott Sutton

Loomed Belt by Adam Lovell

When mounting pieces like suspenders with tabs, make sure that the backing goes down each tab. Also, when doing items like armbands or leg bands, leave enough leather on each end to attach ties. **(Ex. 2.36)** These bands are easily done on the sewing machine but may be hand stitched as well.

Ex. 2.36 Armband by Scott Sutton

Use a whipstitch around the outside warp thread and the leather when mounting loom work by hand. Barrettes, with the barrette blank in between the beadwork and the leather backing, may be hand stitched, or they may be mounted using the edge beading technique discussed in the Appliqué Beadwork section of this book.

Oklahoma Dress Belt. Reddick Collection

Gallery

Belt, Osage - Jerry Smith Collection

Prairie Vest by Adam Lovell - Mike Tucker Collection

Back of vest - Adam Lovell

Belt by Steve Smith - Reddick Collection

Man's Garter, Sac and Fox - Reddick Collection

Man's Dress Belt, Comanche - Reddick Collection

Men's Dress Belts, Oklahoma - Reddick Collection

Straight Dance Belt by Rex Reddick

Man's Otter Dagger, Oklahoma - Jerry Smith Collection

Man's Belt by Steve Smith - Reddick Collection

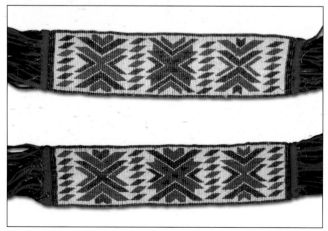

Man's Garters, Chippewa - Reddick Collection

Man's Garters, Potawatomi, Museum of the Great Plains - Tingley Collection

Armband, Oklahoma - Jerry Smith Collection

Belt, Chippewa - Morning Star Gallery

Belt, Oklahoma - Reddick Collection

Armband by Scott Sutton

Bandolier Bag - Private Collection

Belt, Chippewa - Reddick Collection

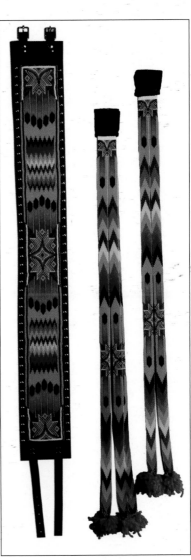

Belt with Matching Side Drops, by Adam Lovell

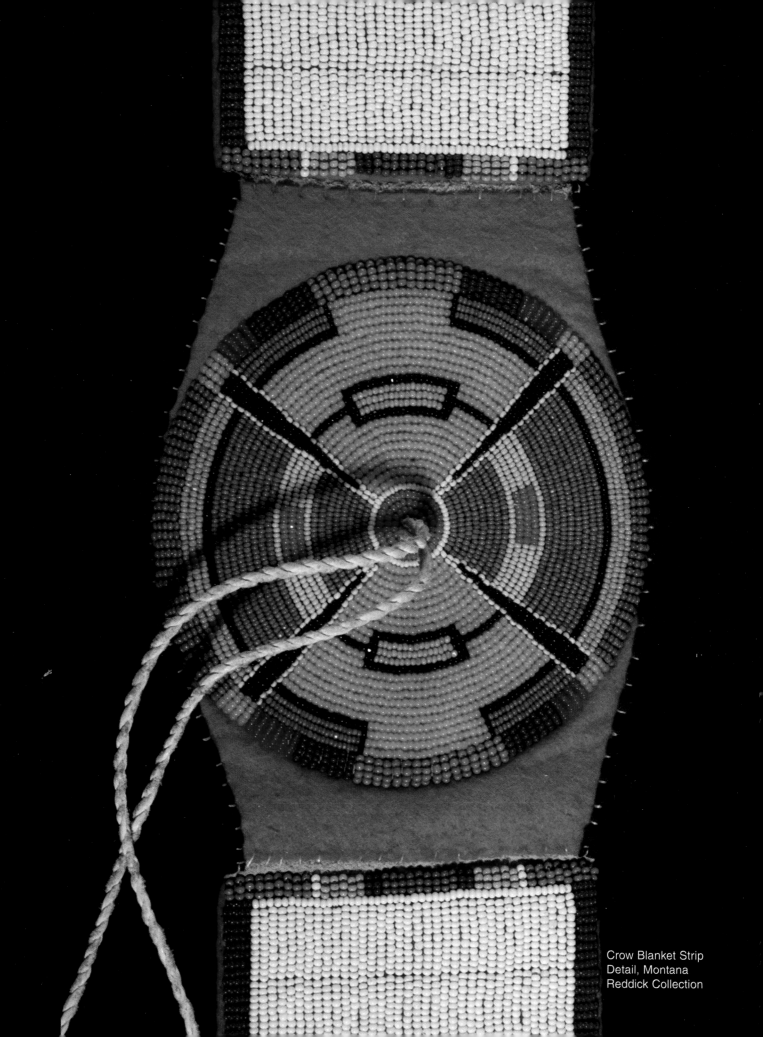

Crow Blanket Strip
Detail, Montana
Reddick Collection

Appliqué Beadwork 3

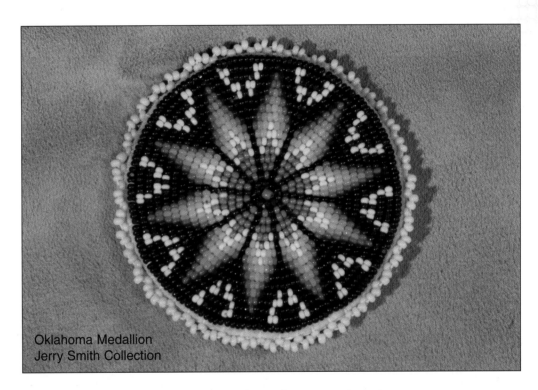

Oklahoma Medallion
Jerry Smith Collection

Appliqué Beadwork:

Two-needle appliqué beadwork is very versatile. It is used to do barrettes, buckles, hair ties, belts, aprons, leggings, purses, medallions, cuffs, armbands, and many other items. There is a one-needle technique, but more typically two needles are used.

Materials:

Beads: A large variety of beads may be used: seed, bugle, iris or hexagon. Bead preference seems to depend on the object, tribal tradition, availability of beads, and the preference of the bead worker. Common bead types for medallions from the Southern Plains are small cut beads 13/0 and smaller, but many are done in 11/0 in both cuts and non-cuts. A lot of Crow appliqué work is done in 11/0 or even larger seed beads. Thread: Nymo size "D" works well. Needles: 12S for smaller beads, 11S for bigger beads. Beeswax. Backing: I prefer a fabric called "Hospital Sheeting" which is available at fabric stores. It is a bonded fabric with two layers of felt and a layer of rubber in the middle. Waterproof baby sheets are the same material. This material is soft, thin, and, when cut, does not ravel. On top of this, use a layer of either 20lb. white paper or butcher paper upon which to outline your design. Other suitable backing materials are canvas, layers of muslin, buckram, or Pellon. When appliqué beadwork decorates an item made of trade cloth, the trade cloth is the backing. Trade cloth (sometimes referred to a broadcloth) is excellent high quality tightly woven wool with a distinctive selvage edge. Historically, this cloth, milled largely for military uniforms, appeared on the early trade lists; thus the name trade cloth.

Seed Bead Color Chart
Opaque Colors:

Silver-Lined Seed Bead

Opaque Seed Bead Examples

Cut Beads Showing Iris, Opaque and Transparent

Black		Dark Brown	
Pearl		Chartreuse	
White		Light Green	
Ivory		Green	
Grey		Turquoise Green	
Pink		Turquoise	
Light Pink		Light Blue	
Coral		Lt. Powder Blue	
Red Orange		Turquoise Blue	
Light Red		Steel Blue	
Red		Periwinkle	
Wine Red		Medium Blue	
Orange		Royal Blue	
Light Orange		Navy Blue	
Yellow		Purple	
Brown		Light Purple	

Transparent Colors:

Crystal		Green	
Grey		Dark Green	
Red		Kelly Green	
Dark Red		Peacock Blue	
Orange		Turquoise Blue	
Yellow		Dark Turquoise	
Amber		Medium Blue	
Topaz		Royal Blue	
Dk. Brown		Dark Montana Blue	
Lt. Green		Dark Purple	

Bugle Beads In Various Lengths

Frames: Some type of frame is needed to support the work while it is in progress. Embroidery hoops, the wooden type with a screw to tighten them, work well. If the project is oddly shaped, you may need to make a wood frame to fit. In this case, thumb tacks or pushpins are used to hold the work on the frame. Some bead workers do not use frames at all. It is a personal choice. I find it much easier to use a frame.

Styles:

Ex. 3.01 Crow Belt - Reddick Collection

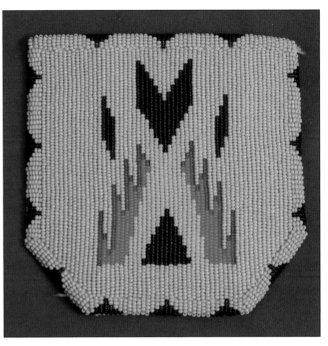

Ex. 3.03 Crow Belt Pouch, Montana. Reddick Collection

There are a few different approaches to creating designs with the appliqué beadwork technique. **(Ex. 3.01 & 3.02)** When doing projects like medallions, barrettes, buckles or hair-ties, two different styles are used. One is a freeform that is used in doing flowers, animals, or other "curvy" shapes. This style features a technique where beads outline basic design elements that are then filled in with other bead rows. The other technique features either concentric circles or a series of parallel lines where the design elements are embedded as part of the rows. The parallel rows run vertically or horizontally, depending on tribal preference. **(Ex. 3.03)**

Clothing items such as aprons, vests, wearing blankets, Osage skirts, etc. are often beaded in the freeform style directly onto trade cloth and sometimes buckskin. The cloth or buckskin becomes the background color. **(Ex. 3.04)** This style, sometimes referred to as Prairie Floral, is characterized by distinct abstract floral elements, color balance, and fill-in schemes. Because of its uniqueness, I recommend the viewing of many examples of this type of work in publications, in collections, or on the internet before drawing up a pattern for a project of this style.

Ex. 3.02 Kiowa Medallion Necklace. B. Hardin Collection

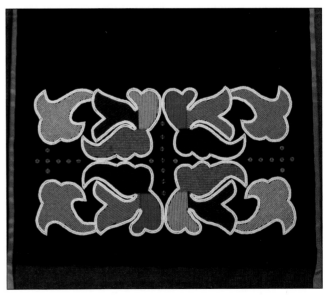

Ex. 3.04 Prairie Applique Beaded Apron. Reddick Collection

Technique:

After deciding on what project you desire - rose, medallion, belt buckle, etc. - draw a design on 20 lb. paper. **(Fig. 1)** If you are doing a medallion, draw only a series of guidelines: the circumference and a series of spokes. **(Fig. 2)** It is a good idea to copy your designs for future use. Secure the backing and paper together in the frame (e.g., an embroidery hoop), making sure it is taut. If it is a large project, it helps to baste the paper to the backing before putting it into the frame.

Thread two needles, one with double thickness and one with single thickness. Wax both threads and tie knots at the ends. The thread with the double thickness will be the one that the beads are strung on. The single thread will be the tack down thread.

Beads may be taken off the hanks and placed in containers, or they may be left on the hanks and used one string at a time. One advantage to working off the hank is realized when a spill occurs, as only a few beads are lost instead of a large quantity.

Depending on the shape you are working on, your technique will vary. When beading a circular medallion, you start in the center and work your way out; conversely, when doing a floral design, you do only the outline first then fill last. With either type, it is very important to remember, DESIGNS MUST HIT/LAND RIGHT ON THE DRAWN LINES AND GUIDE LINES, LETTING THE BACKGROUND FLEX AROUND THE DESIGN. No one is going to count the number of background beads, but they will surely see if you have left out or incorrectly located beads critical in defining the outline. Also, it is very important *not to cram a bead into every space*. Small spaces or voids will never be seen from even a short distance away, and the bonus is that the work will lay flatter. Well done appliqué work lays nice and flat. Crammed beads cause bunching, which will give your work a bumpy appearance. Crammed beads may also cause the design to appear asymmetrical or misshapen, as well as bumpy.

Fig. 1

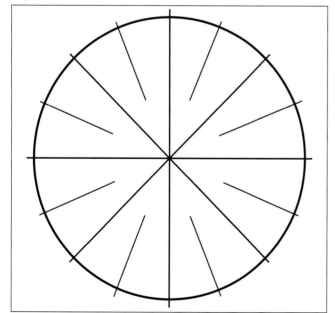

Fig. 2

Example of good, flat applique technique.

Beading Medallions:

After preparing the backing, begin at the center. **(Fig. 3)** The goal of sewing down the first bead is to place it directly over the center point. Using a needle with doubled thread, come through the backing. The needle should poke through the surface a half a bead width from the center point. Place a single bead on the needle and slide it down the thread until it rests on the backing. Push the needle back down through the backing one-half a bead width from the center point across from where you came up. Pull the thread through. It is normal for the beeswax to ball up a little. You've completed your first row!

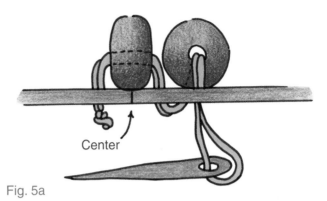

Fig. 5a

The goal for the second row is to create a circle of beads barely touching the center bead. Each bead will be tacked down with stitches that precisely lay on a radius of the circle. **Note:** Some medallions start with a chrome spot in the center, and the first bead row will encircle the spot.

So, to begin the second row, come up with the double threaded needle a half a bead width away from the center bead. **(Fig. 4)** Thread a few beads (7 or 8) on this needle and slide the first bead down to where it meets the backing. With the second single threaded needle (the "tacking" thread), tack down the thread of the first needle by coming up on one side of this double thread and going down on the other side. **(Fig. 5 & 5a)** The tacking stitch must coincide with the radius of the circle. To facilitate this, always keep the double thread at a ninety-degree angle to the bead in the center.

Next, slide the second bead down the thread and into place, coaxing it with the tacking needle. **(Fig. 6)** Slightly move the double thread about the center bead clockwise to maintain that 90-degree angle. Tack down the second thread as with the first. When snugging your tacking thread, do not pull so hard that you buckle the beads.

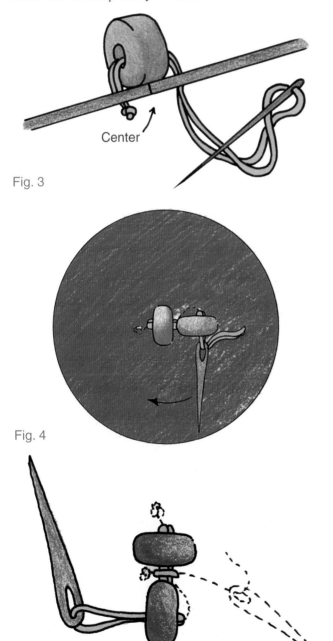

Fig. 3

Fig. 4

Fig. 5

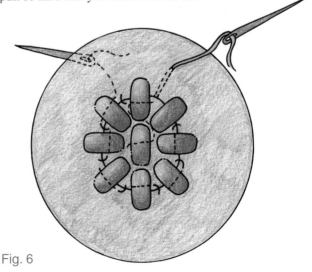

Fig. 6

Continue in this manner up to the last (7th or 8th) bead. The last bead is sewn down by passing the double threaded needle through the first bead of the row, then stitching down through the backing. To be consistent, there should be a tacking stitch between the last bead and the first, although it is not necessary. As you sew down each bead, note whether it falls in position directly over your design lines. If not, you may have to substitute a bead of a different size.

Starting with row 3, and in successive rows, there will be a tacking stitch between every two beads and not between each bead. However, when you get out to rows 5 or 6, every three beads may be sewn down. Never sew more than three beads at a time. Doing so will cause the work to pucker and buckle. Again, the work needs to lay flat. When you examine the best quality medallions, every two beads have been tacked down.

Here is an extremely important question to ask: "How do you keep the critical points of the design lined up exactly on the guide lines?" Answer: "It all has to do with bead selection." This means that sometimes you have to pick out thinner beads or fatter beads to make sure you stay exactly on the lines. Fewer divisions of the circle are desirable when you first start out until you get the hang of keeping the design on the lines. Pick 8 divisions as opposed to 16. Never string the entire row of beads on at one time. You never know when a thinner or fatter bead will be needed. Even the thread thickness of the tacking stitches adds to the length of the string of beads as you go along. As a beginner, it is best to put only enough beads on to go from one guideline to the next. This will save you from taking off beads and making countless adjustments. The exception to this is if the row is of one solid color, then it makes no difference whether the beads hit the guidelines or not. So, string away, and happy tacking.

Continue working until you have completed the medallion to the desired size. Don't be over-zealous at first. Keep the diameter down to 1.5" or less until you have the technique down well, then you can go for bigger medallions with more complex design elements. There is no way to teach someone just starting out how to do complex Native-looking patterns. Start with the simple designs and progress to the more intricate. Experienced bead workers produce very artistic, dramatic, and imaginative medallions with excellent contrast and symmetry. The medallions pictured here illustrate these qualities. Viewing as many medallions as possible will help you to modify and create your own designs. Though we

often say that "copying is the sincerest form of flattery," it is important that you do not copy beadwork designs of others. (Some designs are considered proprietary "family designs".)

Once the beadwork for the medallion is complete, it needs to be backed and edge beaded. (At this point, we are just making a medallion, so we are not going to be concerned with placing hardware such as buckle blanks or barrettes into the backing.) Using Aleene's Tacky Glue®, spread a thin layer of glue over the entire back of the medallion just inside the last row. Do not allow the glue to ooze past the next to last row. Place the beadwork against the piece of leather that will be used as the final backing. Thin buckskin is best, though felt, canvas, or ultra suede can be used for this purpose as well. If the medallion needs a pair of ties, they need to be threaded through two holes punched in the center of the leather backing before it is glued to the medallion. After the backing is applied, the work is freed from the hoop. Putting the medallion under a couple of heavy books as the glue dries will make it nice and flat. Once the glue is set, trim off the excess leather and paper backing close to the beadwork, but don't cut the threads! Edge beading will be the final step in completing the medallion.

Edge Beading:

There are two general techniques of using beads to finish the edge of a piece of beadwork: one is called picot edging, and the other is whip-stitch edging. On the simple medallions just discussed, one of the picot styles known as two- bead edging is common, though there are several forms of picot edging.

Picot and Whip Stitch Edging

Two-Bead Edging:

Using a single needle, thread it double, wax it, and tie both ends together with a knot. Use the needle to pierce up from the leather back of the medallion to the beadwork side and extremely close to the last bead row. The needle should come out between the outside edge of the last bead row and the backing edge. Do not come up between the beads of the last row. String on three beads, and stitch from back to front approximately 2 bead widths away. After making the stitch, go back up through the last bead and snug the thread. **(Fig. 7)** This will make the third bead lay flat against the edge of the medallion, and it will make the second bead stand up. Next, put on another 2 beads. Sew back-to-front, then back up through the second bead and snug the thread. Uniform stitches about two bead widths apart are important to get the middle bead to stand propped up on the other two. If the stitches are too far apart, the middle bead will sink down and touch the edge of the medallion. This is not correct. Yet, if the stitches are too close together, "beads #1 and #3" will touch, and this is unacceptable. Continue beading around the medallion edge by putting two beads on at a time until you are within one bead of the first bead of the edging. To complete the edging, place one bead on the needle and go down through the first bead of the picot edging pushing the needle through the leather backing. **(Fig. 8)** To finish, tie off the thread.

If, for some reason, your thread comes up short and you need to stop and start a new thread in the middle, this is what you do. Put the two beads on as you have been doing, except this time go from the front to the back. Pull the thread all the way through and cut the needle loose. You should have a tail of about three inches left for tying it to the new thread. Rethread your needle, wax it, but do not knot it. About 1/16" away from where the thread left as a tail pokes out, stick the needle into the backing and thrust the point through the backing so its point comes up through the second bead. Now, pull the thread through to within 3 inches of its end. Tie the tail of the first thread to the tail of the new one. **(Fig. 9)** Use a knot that will not slip, and trim the tails. After knotting, continue edge beading.

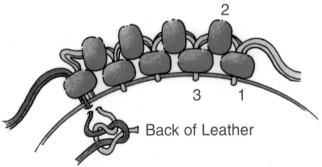

Fig. 9

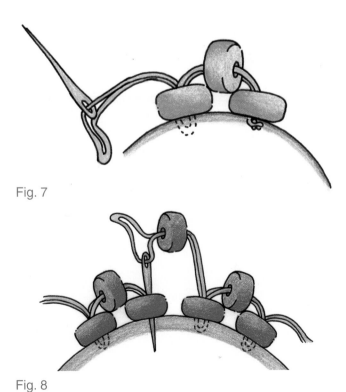

Fig. 7

Kiowa Medallion, Oklahoma. B. Hardin Collection

Fig. 8

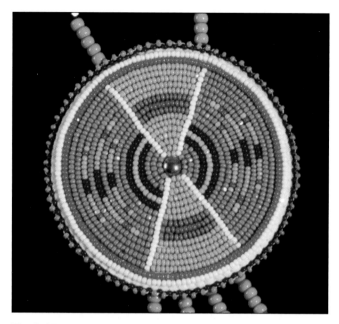

Ex. 3.05 Crow Medallion, Montana. J. Reddick Collection

Two-bead edging (**Ex. 3.05**) is just one of many variations of picot edging. The following pictures illustrate some of the more prevalent: 1-bead stack, 2-bead stack, 1/2/3/2/1 stack, 3-bead picot, 4-loop, 5-bead loop and even two row picot. (**Fig. 10 A thru. G**)

Fig. 10-C: 2-Bead stack varition.

Fig. 10-D: 1-2-3-2-1 Bead stack.

Fig. 10-A: 1-Bead Stack.

Fig. 10-E: 3-Bead loops.

Fig. 10-B: 2-Bead Stack.

Fig. 10-F: 4-Bead loops.

Fig. 10-G: Double Picot Edging

Ex. 3.06   Applique Belt Buckle with whip-stitch edging - by Scott Sutton.

Whip-Stitch Edging:

There is a second method that may be used to do the edge work. Most often this technique is used on belt buckles, purses or dance items such as cuffs. If you choose this technique, you must leave a border of background material completely around the beaded object of at least 1/8" and up to ¼".

Using a needle with double thread, tie a small knot in the end. Come up through the backing (from the back) at the edge of the beadwork. **(Fig. 11)** Put enough beads on the thread to cover the front and back of the un-beaded edge. Make a whip-stitch over the edge and back up through the backing so that the needle pierces the backing a bead length away from the initial stitch in the backing. Snug the thread. Bead the second row by putting on the same number of beads as the first row, whip-stitch over, pull the needle out one bead away from the previous stitch and snug the thread. Continue in this manner until the entire project is edged.

By symmetrically marking the border around the object, you can create a banded edge with different colors. **(Ex. 3.06)** Alternating the colors used in adjacent rows may create a striped border. For example: 4 rows of background color, two rows of a darker color. Borders may be done in a solid color.

When the thread becomes too short to continue, end it by stitching into and out of the backing several times, then cut the thread. Start a new thread as before and continue on. To finish, stitch in and out of the backing in between the first and last row to hide your stitches, then cut the thread.

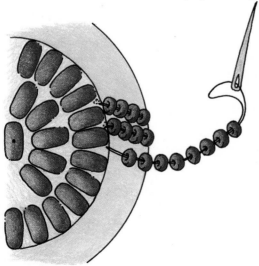

Fig. 11   Whip-Stitch Edging

Ex. 3.06a   Detail view of whip stitch edging on Crow Cuff - by Scott Sutton

Belt Buckle Backing:

To make a beaded belt buckle, a metal plate known as a buckle blank must be attached to the backing. These may be obtained from any quality trader and come in a variety of shapes and sizes. **(Ex. 3.07)** The beadwork is done to fit the shape of the buckle blank.

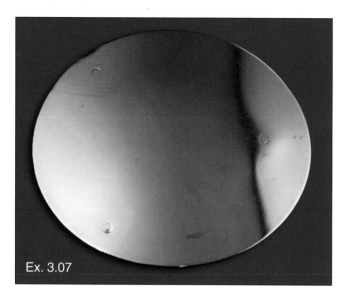

Ex. 3.07

To begin construction, trace around the buckle onto a piece of paper. Then, with a ruler, mark outside the perimeter by 1/8". You now have two lines on the paper. The first (inside line) will be the outside edge of the beadwork piece. The second (the outside line) extends 1/8" past the edge of the buckle and will become the edgework area where the buckle will be sewed together using the edge beading technique of whipstitching. I also place several grid lines on the paper dividing it in half vertically and horizontally, as well as a few others. Once this is done, I make copies of this so I don't have to do it again for other buckles of this size. These lines help me keep my design centered and oriented.

Perform the beadwork as I did with the medallion, described above. Briefly, this involves placing the paper and a piece of hospital sheeting in a frame, such as an embroidery hoop, and using the paper guidelines to sew beads directly onto the sheeting.

Once the beadwork is complete, remove the beaded material from your frame and trim it to the outside perimeter mark (1/8" from the edge of the beadwork) but not all the way to the beadwork's edge. Now glue the buckle blank to the back of the beaded sheeting with Aleene's Tacky Glue. Spread a thin layer of glue on the sheeting, coming close to the edge of the beadwork. Let it dry for a couple of minutes, then press it onto the metal buckle blank. Make sure your bead

work is centered on the blank and that, if it is a pictograph or some design that has a certain orientation, the beadwork is mounted so that the buckle may be used in the standard fashion of belts. Allow the glue to dry.

Next, leather backing must be put on. Cut a piece of leather the same general shape as the buckle but approximately 1/2" wider all the way around. Turn the buckle with its back facing toward you, **(Ex. 3.08)** then lay the leather over it so that the blank is fairly centered under the leather. Feel for the hook and mark a corresponding dot on the leather, then punch a hole for the hook part of the blank.

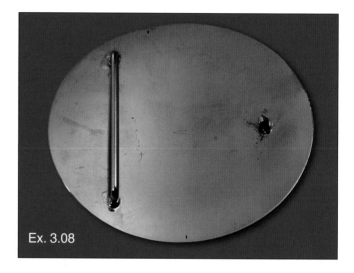

Ex. 3.08

Place the leather back onto the blank with the hook through the hole, then fold the leather back where the leather meets the metal bar. Mark the leather at the spots where the ends of the bar are soldered to the blank, then punch two holes in the leather. Make cuts from the outside edge of the leather to the holes. **(Ex. 3.09)**

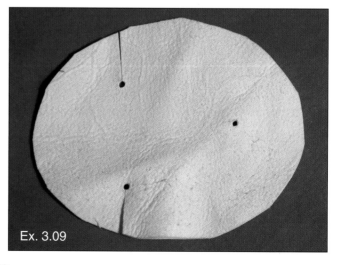

Ex. 3.09

Put glue on the buckle blank and work the leather under the belt bar and over the hook. Press this firmly and allow it to dry before proceeding. **(Ex. 3.10)** Then, trim away the excess leather and beadwork backing up to the 1/8" outside line that was drawn. Complete the project by edge beading using the whipstitch technique described earlier for edge beading.

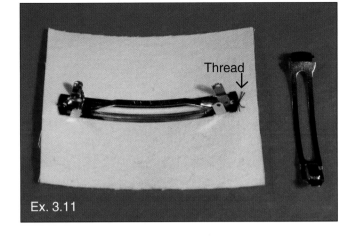
Ex. 3.11

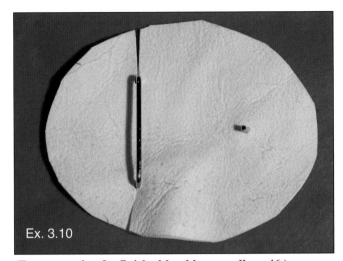
Ex. 3.10

(For a sample of a finished buckle see gallery 46.)

Next, punch 3 sets of holes according to the impressions: 2 holes for the clasp uprights, 2 holes at either end of the hinge, and a hole at each end of the stabilizer bar. Now cut between the two holes for the hinge and make another cut to connect the two holes of the stabilizer bar. Do not cut between the holes for the clasp end, as you can simply push these tabs up through the two holes you punched as you push the other pieces up through the holes and slits you cut for them. **(Ex. 3.12)**

Barrettes:

I recommend using a quality metal barrette blank acquired from a reputable trader. I prefer the French made barrettes, as they are better constructed than others. Do not use the plastic or cheap metal ones, as they will not hold up.

With the methods described previously, use paper and hospital sheeting in a frame to do the beadwork. For barrettes, leave a border of 1/2" - 3/4" after you remove the beadwork from the frame and trim away excess material.

Separate the arm from the hinge and set it aside for now. Sew the base section of the barrette to the beadwork piece making sure that it is centered in all directions. **(Ex. 3.11)** Do this by using the holes on each end of the barrette to tack it with thread to the beadwork and tie secure knots.

Next, punch small holes in the leather backing material for the hinge, clasp, and stabilizer bar. Find these locations by laying the leather over the back of the barrette, then pressing down on the upright hinge ends, the two uprights from the clasp, and the length of the stabilizer bar. Firm pressing will leave indentations in the leather.

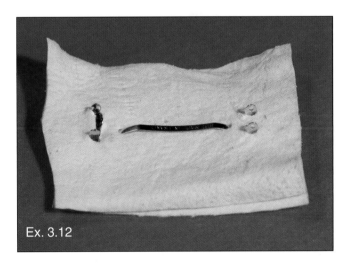
Ex. 3.12

Using Aleene's Tacky Glue and with leather the base section attached, spread glue on the back of the beadwork piece almost to the edge. Make sure that glue also gets on the metal of the barrette but not on the hinge or clasp. Glue the leather backing over the hinge, clasp, and stabilizer bar. Press down until the backing is smooth. Then, reattach the arm to the hinge. At this point, you can proceed to trim off the extra backing material close to the edge of the beadwork as mentioned earlier and begin edge beading the project.

Freeform Appliqué:

Fig. 12

A second style of doing appliqué is more of a freeform style employing many of the same techniques used in doing the medallion. **(Fig. 12)** The big difference is that the outline and other defining lines or curves are beaded first. If you are doing a rose, each petal of the rose and other critical features are the first things beaded. **(Ex. 3.13)** Consider when you were younger and enjoyed coloring books. The big heavy black lines outlined the object and you colored in between the lines. Freeform appliqué is similar: once the outline is beaded, you fill in the outline with other beads. Some tribal styles (e.g., Otoe) incorporate a double white row of outline. When doing the freeform style, you must always tack down every two beads of any outline. Never sew down every three. You will even find it necessary to tack every bead sometimes, particularly if you a navigating a tight corner.

Ex. 3.13   Crow Man's Cuffs - by Scott Sutton

In appliqué work, there are several ways to fill the background. One way is to follow the outline of the object. Of course, as you bead towards the center, the shape is transformed to something that vaguely resembles the original outline shape. Again, it is extremely important not to crowd the beads. This will cause bunching. It is okay to have small gaps. When you hold the object away from you, the gaps will seem to disappear. But, if you crowd the beads and cause buckling, this will be very noticeable.

A second way to fill in outlined objects is to bead in parallel lines. This is very prominent in Prairie floral examples. From shape to shape, the parallel rows do not need to have the same orientation unless there is a matching shape in the design. In most cases, the parallel rows run perpendicular to the longest dimension of the design element. **(Ex. 3.14)**

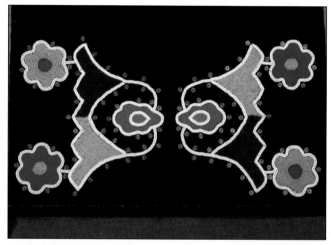

Ex. 3.14a   Detail View of Prairie Apron exhibiting the parallel fill-in technique.   Reddick Collection

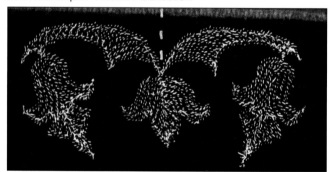

Ex. 3.14b   Apron back, detali of stitching.

If the item is to be fully beaded, the entire background is beaded in parallel rows. These rows almost always run horizontally. Some backgrounds may be filled with a combination of ways due to the shape, size and style of the item. Though there are interlocking rows, parallel rows, and concentric rows in this piece, they are never crowded, and they lay flat. **(Ex. 3.15)**

Ex. 3.15 Detail of parallel rows of beads used to fill-in the background color.

Gallery

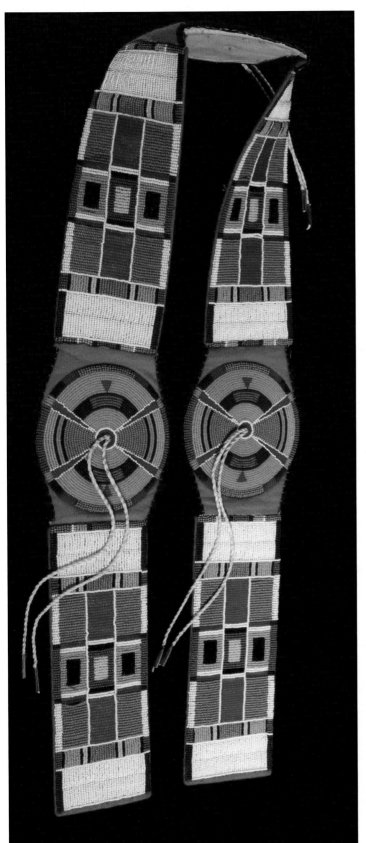

Crow Man's Cuffs, Jerry Smith Collection

Blackfoot Knife Sheath. Sinew Beaded with 18/0 Beads. B. Hardin Collection

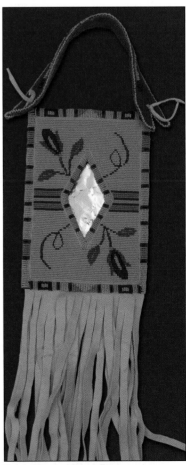

Crow Man's Mirror Bag
Custer Battlefield Trading Post Collection

Crow Style Blanket Strip. Reddick Collection

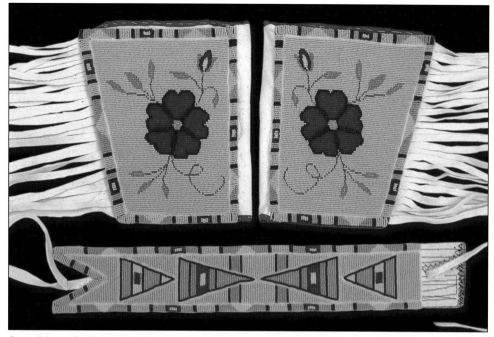

Crow Men's Cuffs and Armband, Custer Battlefield Trading Post Collection

Crow, Tobacco Bag - CBTP Collection

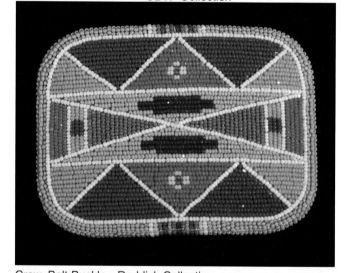

Matching Medallions by Fern Sluder, Kiowa - Reddick Collection

Crow, Belt Buckle - Reddick Collection

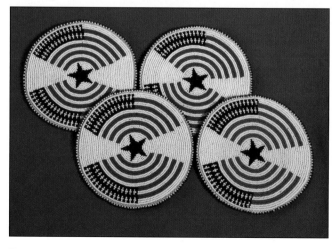

Crow Belt Pouches, Custer Battlefield Trading Post Collection

Tipi Medallions by Fern Sluder, Kiowa - Reddick Collection

Medallion, Oklahoma - Jerry Smith Collection

Barrette   Barrette

by Scott Sutton

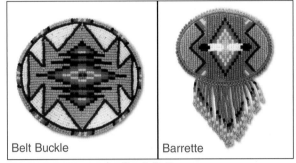

Belt Buckle   Barrette

by Scott Sutton

Plateau, Beaded Bags - Private Collection

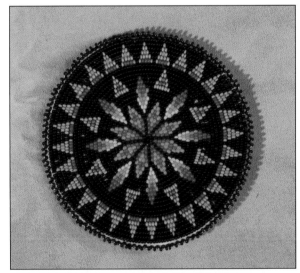

Medallion, Oklahoma - Jerry Smith Collection

Crow, Lance Case - CBTP Collection

Crow, Appliqued Belt - Reddick Collection

47

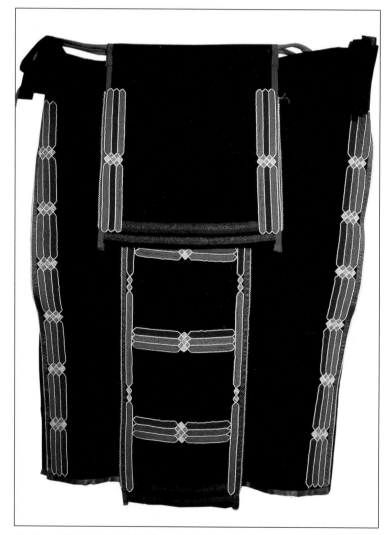

Medallion, Oklahoma - Private Collection

Applique Beaded Straight Dance Suit, Osage Style -
Jerry Smith Collection

Beaded Bolos, Sioux - Richard Green Collection

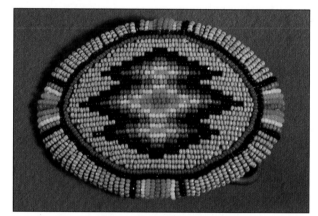

Belt Buckle, Oklahoma - Reddick Collection

Medallion Necklace, Oklahoma - Reddick Collection

Bag, Plateau Style - by Scott Sutton

Medallion, Oklahoma - Reddick Collection

Barrette, Oklahoma - Reddick Collection

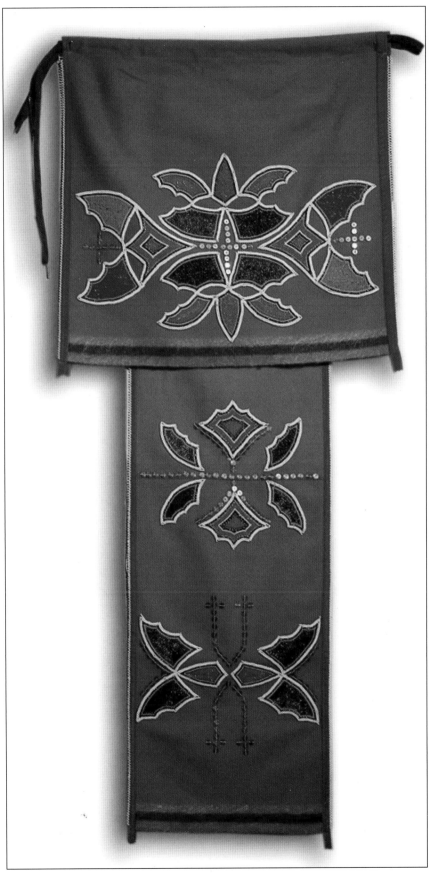

Man's Apron and Trailer, by Carl Jennings - Jerry Smith Collection

Peyote Beadwork

Peyote Gourd Rattles. Reddick Collection

Peyote beadwork is a most often style used when beading cylindrical or three dimensional objects. It is a type of netted beadwork, meaning that each bead is interlaced with other beads. Fan handles, rattle handles, feather shafts, dance sticks, bolo ties and earrings are just some of the items beaded in this style. The technique described here is called the 3-drop method, based on the trio of beads formed in the netting process.

The term "peyote beadwork" comes from the practice of beading many items associated with the Peyote Church (aka Native American Church) with this technique. Another term applied to the same style is " gourd stitch", referring to the beaded gourd rattles used in this religion.

Materials:

Beads: 13/0 Charlotte cut beads are quite common, but many items are done in non-cut beads or a combination of cut and non-cut. 12/0 and now 11/0 cut are also common. Older Native American Church pieces and items of small diameters make use of very small 15/0, 16/0 or even smaller beads. Though these are extremely small beads, the time and patience it takes to decorate an item with such small beads make it highly treasured. Cut beads, though more expensive, are often preferred, as they sparkle in the light as rays bounce off the facets of the bead.

Thread: Nymo size "A" or "B" for smaller beads. Size "D" for 11/0 beads. Needles: 12 Sharps are best. If using smaller beads, you may even need a smaller needle. Be prepared: These needles break easily. Beeswax: Just enough to coat the thread. You don't want it to be gummy; that will clog the beads. Backing: Very thin leather or ultra suede should be used to cover the project before work is started. Miscellaneous: Sharp scissors; flat-bladed pliers may be used to break a bead.

Technique:

As with the previous beading techniques, mastery of peyote beadwork takes lots of practice. Starting the 3-drop peyote style of beadwork is one of the most difficult beading techniques to learn; so, it is prudent to practice on a small object such as a plastic pen or a wooden dowel about / − 3/8" in diameter before moving on to the beading an entire dance stick. Creating designs is also a challenge to those just starting. The accompanying photos show contrasting zigzag color bands, "rainbow" lines (dream lines), feathers, hexagons, flags, etc. These are very common motifs in peyote beaded items. There is some 3-drop peyote graph paper included in this book to help you map out designs based on the photos in this section.

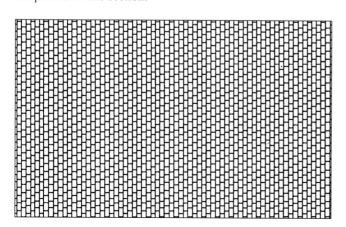

The following example explains how to bead a small dowel from bottom to top: To begin, the object to be beaded must be covered with thin leather or ultra-suede. The leather will make the surface somewhat non-skid, allowing the beads to lay on their edges without shifting. Any bump on the surface of the backing will produce a bump on the completed beadwork, so it is important when gluing the leather on to avoid a ridge/bump from any overlapping edges. There is a little trick to doing this. Cut the leather or ultra suede to the correct length but a little wider than needed. Spread a thin layer of Aleene's® Original Tacky Glue or craft glue completely over one side of the leather or ultra suede. (Ex. 4.01) With the glued side in, wrap the dowel with the leather, and crimp the excess edges together with either your fingernails or pliers. (Ex. 4.02) Wipe off any excess glue, and it is okay to crimp more than once. Let it start to dry for just 2 or 3 minutes. Then, with very sharp scissors, trim off the excess backing. (Ex. 4.03) Smooth down the seam with your fingers, and roll it back and forth (seam down) on a flat surface. (Ex. 4.04) Some bead workers sew this seam together, though sewing tends to create a slight ridge. The reliability of the adhesives today makes sewing unnecessary.

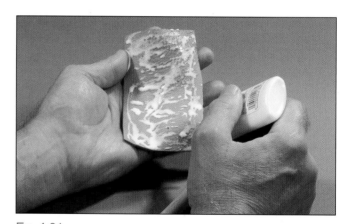

Ex. 4.01

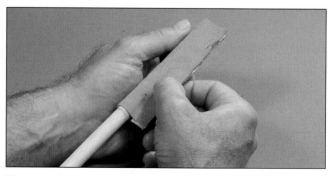

Ex. 4.02

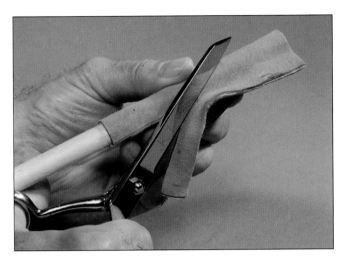

Ex. 4.03

Starting in what will be a background area of the beadwork, insert the needle in and out of the backing at the bottom of the dowel. Pull the thread through until stopped by the knot. **(Ex. 4.05)** This is one style of beadwork where it works best to have the beads loose in a small flat container of some type. String exactly enough beads on the thread to circle the entire object once with no overlap. **(Ex. 4.06)** Getting to this exact number may take 2 or 3 trial and error wrappings along with the removing and adding of beads. Now for the math: Count the number of beads it takes to go around. Most of the Native design elements require this number to be evenly divisible by 6: like 12, 18, 24, 30, 36, etc. So, what happens if the total number of beads around the object is 33? Round the number up. Do not round down. Thirty-six will be the total number of beads used in this example.

Once the glue under the backing has dried, mark off guidelines. Minimally, mark the center of the piece. Other marks may be made where you want design elements to start. Thread a 12 Sharps needle with a single thickness of Nymo thread. Only one thickness is used, as the thread will pass through each bead twice. Use the appropriate size of thread for the size of beads you are using. Wax the thread enough to coat it, but not so much that it will be scraped off the thread when you go through a bead. Finally, tie an overhand knot at the end of the thread and clip off the tail.

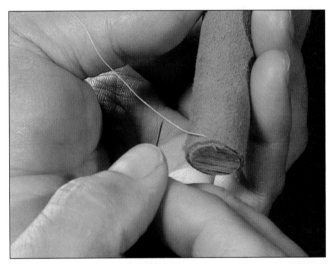

Ex. 4.05

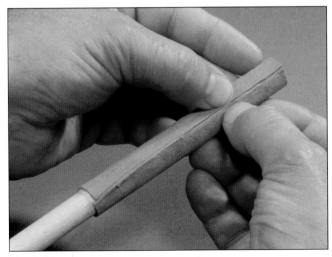

Ex. 4.04

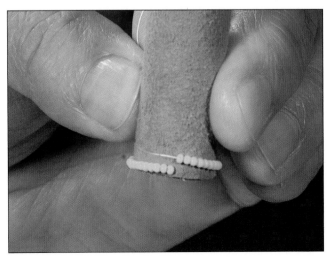

Ex. 4.06

Remove one-third of the beads. With 36 beads, you take off 12 beads, leaving 24 on the thread. Wrap the thread with the beads on it around the object clockwise if you are right handed. "Leftys" can go counter clockwise. Then pass the needle back through the first bead. **(Ex. 4.07)** From here on, tension is important. It needs to be maintained at all times. Usually the hand holding the object being beaded helps maintain the tension, which should be maintained in the direction you are going.

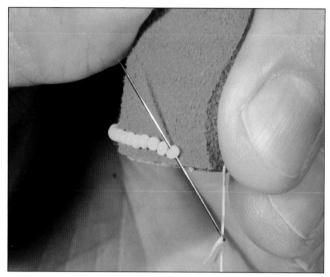

Ex. 4.07

The following example is for the right-handed crafter: So that you can distinguish the second row from the first 24 beads, a different color (red) is used. Put one red bead on the needle. Skip bead #2 and go through bead #3 of the first 24, entering the bead from the right. Keep the thread on the up side of the object as you pull it snug. When snug, you will see the new colored bead (red) staggered higher and nestled between beads #2 and #3. **(Ex. 4.08)**

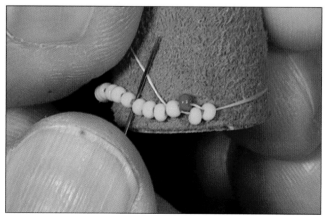

Ex. 4.08

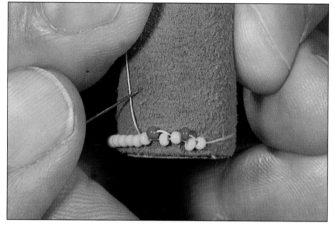

Ex. 4.09

Keep up the slight tension on the thread as you put another bead on the needle. Skip the 4th bead and go through the 5th bead. As you continue in this manner, there will be two yellow beads between each red bead. **(Ex. 4.09)** You will find it necessary to position beads with your fingernail. Space or slot them into the proper position until they look like the beads in the photo. Remember to keep the tension. When the last bead of the row is on the needle, #12 (red), it is netted into place the same as the others except after going through bead #1 in row 1, go through the first red bead of row 2. **(Ex. 4.10)** In other words, you must go through two beads to end the row. This will position the thread to start row 3. Thirty-six beads now have been put in place.

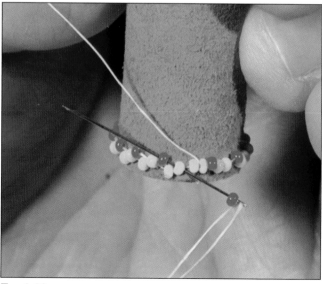

Ex. 4.10

For ease in visualization, another contrasting color is used for the next row so that you will easily be able to see the beadwork layout. There is no design being made at this time; the basic technique is just being detailed. Begin row #3 by putting on one green bead and going through the second red bead. **(Ex. 4.11)** Put on another green bead, and go through the next red bead on the left, meaning the next bead of row two. Continue in this manner with the other remaining (9) green beads. The last green bead, #12, will be netted into place by passing through a red bead (the #1 red bead) and the #1 green bead. **(Ex. 4.12)** Again, you pass through two beads to end the row, as you will do when ending every subsequent row. As you end the row, a little extra "tug in your snug" would be a good thing.

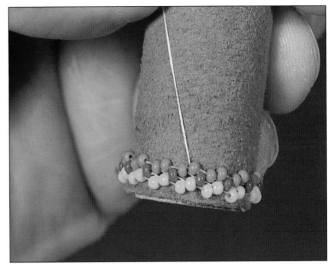

Ex. 4.13

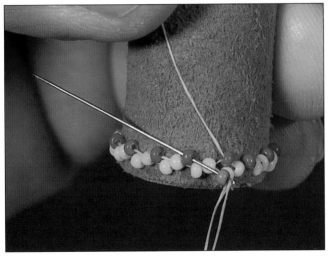

Ex. 4.11

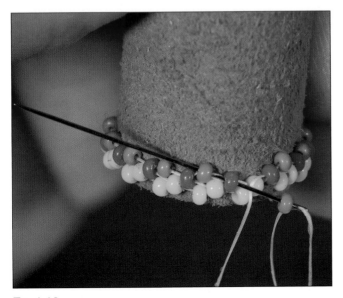

Ex. 4.12

Do the fourth row with 12 green beads just as you did the third. Viewing the piece, at this juncture, you will see 5 beads slanting to the right and 3 beads (yellow, red, green) going to the left. **(Ex. 4.13)** Since it takes three rows to completely net 36 beads around the cylinder, the trio of beads in the yellow/red/green formation indicates why it is called the 3-drop style.

Well, there you have it: the basic peyote beading technique. Though starting is complicated to explain, putting on one bead at a time is not hard, just time consuming. It should be noted that you can start anywhere in the section to be peyote beaded as you can bead up and then turn the item over and then continue beading up. "Over" means to exchange the top with the bottom. The diagonal spiral created with the peyote technique will still be going down right to left.

As mentioned above, the zigzag is a very common design element in peyote beadwork, and though most of this book is based on technique, it would be unfair not to explain details of this pattern.

Using the background color (green in the photos) as one color and a second color (yellow in this case), this is how the basic zigzag is created: It takes 5 rows to complete one zigzag element.

Zigzag Design Element

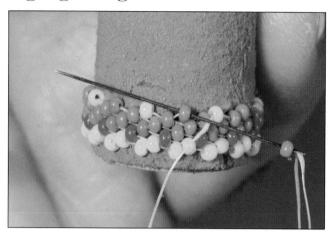

Ex. 4.14

Row #1 - First, put on a yellow bead and then a green, alternating colors as you net all 12 beads. **(Ex. 4.14)**

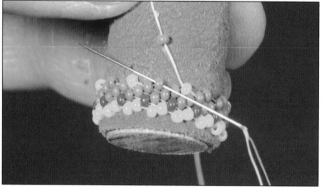

Ex. 4.15

Row #2 – The first bead of this row is green. Next, put on a yellow bead, then a green and continue to alternate until you have put on 12 beads. **(Ex. 4.15, 4.16 & 4.17)**

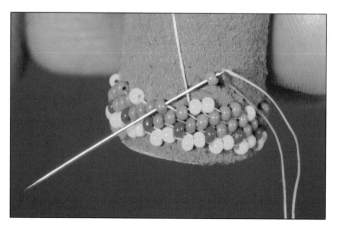

Ex. 4.16

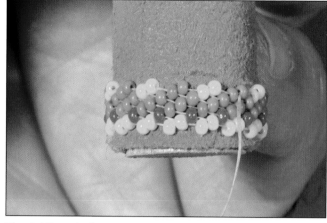

Ex. 4.17 end of row

Row #3 - Put on 12 yellow beads. A "V" formation emerges with the yellow beads from rows #1, #2 and #3. **(Ex. 4.18)**

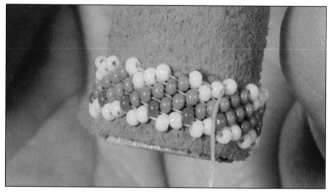

Ex. 4.18

Row #4 - Again, on this row, you will alternate bead colors, green and yellow. Make sure the green bead nestles in the vertex of the "V." **(Ex. 4.19)**

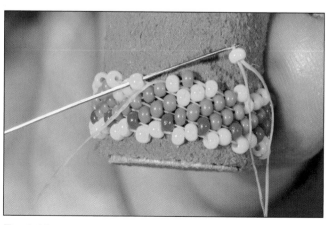

Ex. 4.19

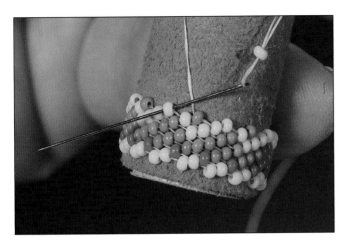

Ex. 4.20

Row #5 – Alternate colors again, making sure the yellow is next to the yellow of the previous row and green is next to green. **(Ex. 4.20)**

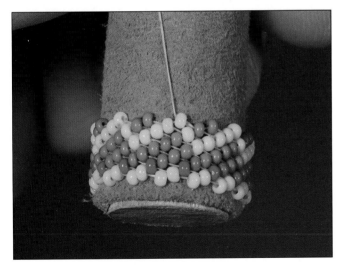

Ex. 4.21

When Row #5 is completed, you will be able to see the zigzag with 5 yellow beads going to the right and 3 yellow beads going to the left. **(Ex. 4.21)** Understanding this basic zigzag will open the doors for many interesting designs. For instance, a more dramatic zigzag would start out with one yellow and two green, one yellow and two green – four sets of these. It is fairly easy to see that a nested set of zigzags in rainbow colors can be formed by picking a new color to be slotted into the vertex of the "V" (row #4) whenever it appears.

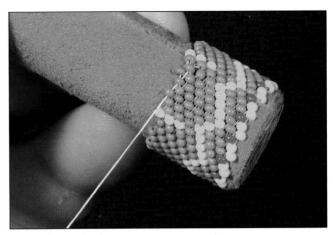

Ex. 4.22

Okay, if you had the instruction for one more design element, the door would be open even wider. It is a simple one: a vertical line. Let's use the yellow and green, where the background is green. **(Ex. 4.22)**

Gourd Rattle Handles. Reddick Collection

Vertical Line

Row #1 - One yellow, 2 green, one yellow, 2 green – until all 12 are netted. (**Ex. 4.23 & 4.24**)

Row #2 - 12 green

Row #3 – 12 green

Row #4 – One yellow, two green, one yellow, 2 green – until all 12 are netted (**Ex. 4.25**)

Row #5 – 12 green

Row #6 – 12 green

Row #7 – One yellow, two green, one yellow, 2 green – until all 12 are netted (**Ex. 4.26**)

Ex. 4.26

(**Ex. 4.27**) As the photo shows, you end up with a series of vertical lines composed of 3 yellow beads each. Carrying this pattern just a few more rows will make the vertical lines longer. If you vary the colors of the vertical line you will get "dream lines" (lines with a rainbow-like graduation of colors).

Ex. 4.23

Ex. 4.27

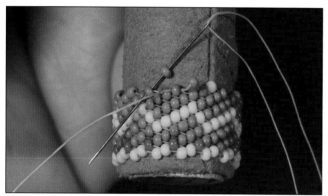

Ex. 4.24

If you combine the zigzag with the vertical lines, you may create hexagons. It is not much of a stretch to see how black and white tail feathers may be created.

Getting back to more practical matters, suppose you have to end a thread because it is getting too short and you need to continue on. It is best to do this when you have ended a row (though this is not imperative). After ending a row (remember the extra tug in your snug), stitch into the backing material 3 – 5 times and cut the thread close to the leather backing. (**Fig. 1**) It is not recommended that you weave the thread back through previously netted beads, as the extra woven thread may be slightly visible, and there is the potential of breaking a bead. To start the new thread, knot it, stitch into the backing very close to the last row and go through any bead in the last row nearest the stitch. You are ready to continue beading. (**Fig. 2**)

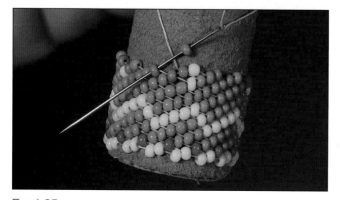

Ex. 4.25

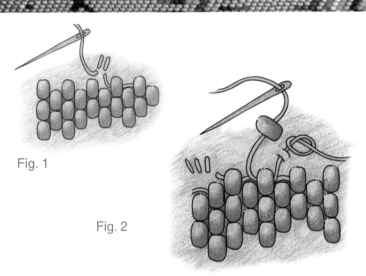

Fig. 1

Fig. 2

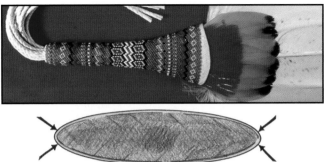

Fig. 3 Fan handle cross-section. Add beads at arrows

At the very end, following the euphoria you experience from netting the last bead in place, run the thread through all the beads of the last row. Snug the thread a little tighter than normal, and then thread the needle through the adjacent diagonal of 3-5 beads. Pull hard enough on the thread so that, when it is clipped right off at the bead surface, the very short "tail" will be sucked back in and hidden by the beads.

Adding Beads:

One more useful technique needs to be discussed in this chapter on peyote beadwork, and that is the process of adding beads. When doing items such as tapering flat fan handles, beads will need to be added from time to time to accommodate the expanding circumference of the taper. Beads should always be added in the background and at both sides of the tapering portion. Adding beads in the background and to the side will make this disruption of the 3-drop formation a less noticeable transition.

When the phrase "adding beads" is mentioned, it should also be said that the fan handle is being beaded from the bottom to the top. Do not add beads until the object's circumference starts to get bigger.

While working in the background color and netting the non-tapered part of the handle, set aside any thin beads until you start to add beads. These thinner beads will make the transition of adding beads look better.

You want the addition to be symmetrical; so, for a tapered flat fan, two or four beads will be added to the row where the circumference is getting too big. This will depend on the severity or the taper. One bead will be added on the left just as you turn the corner, another just opposite this on the back left, a third on the back side right just as you turn the corner and the forth on the front right side opposite the third. **(Fig. 3)**

Let's assume the thread is in the front center of the row where beads are to be added. When you reach the left side curve, place two thin beads on the needle and net them in as if they were one bead. Then proceed netting as normal with one bead for one or two more beads, depending on the width of the fan. Then, put two more thin beads on and net them in place as if they were one. Continue around the back and across the flat surface until you reach the curve of the other side. Here you will again add two beads in two different places on the rounded edge, just as on the left. End the row as usual by going through two beads so you are ready to begin the next row.

Bead as normal on the next row until you come to the spot where the first thin beads were placed. Though they were sewn in as one bead, treat them here as two single beads now and net a single thin bead between the two. Do this in each of the three other places around the row. This will expand the number of beads in the row by four once the row is complete. The beads may be a little bunchy at first, but this is okay. The bunched beads will lay flat as successive rows are netted in place and as the circumference continues to enlarge.

After this expansion by four beads, you can begin your design again. If the object tapers more severely, it may be necessary to repeat this adding of four beads before starting your design. Never add an odd number of beads to each side. For example, if you added three to a side because it is a steep slant, this will throw off your designs.

Some bead workers prefer to start beading on the wider end of the fan and subtract beads instead of adding beads as the circumference decreases. To subtract beads, you do the reverse of adding. When beads get too tight, skip a total of four beads in the positions on the side curve in the same places you would add beads. There will be gaps at first, but they will be pulled in as you continue the work. Personally, I have found that subtracting beads is more difficult than adding; I would much rather add.

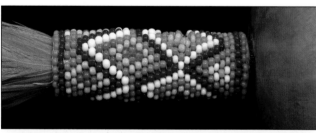

Ex. 4.28 Peyote Gourd Rattle beaded in brickwork technique.
Reddick Collection

Brickwork: See page 59 "Adding Beads

An interesting variation on peyote beadwork is called brickwork or brick stitch. **(Ex. 4.28)** As you might expect from
the name, the beads are applied so that they lay horizontally
instead of vertically. Further, the beads on the second row
lay centered over the spaces between the beads on the first
row, just like bricks **(Ex. 4.29)** The design elements are
essentially the same as 3-drop, including diamonds, parallel-
ograms, zig-zags, triangles, etc. Brickwork goes a little bit
slower than 3-drop, and perhaps that is why it has never
been as popular with Indian artists. Consequently, examples
are seen less frequently than 3-drop.

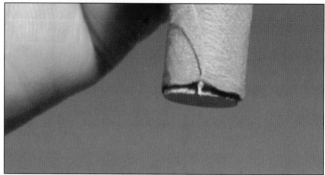

Ex. 4.30

As with any peyote beading, it is best to first cover the
object to be beaded (in this example, a dowel, beaded from
bottom to top) with thin leather or ultra-suede. To start, you
will bead a first row that is referred to as a Ladder.
String a needle with thread and tie a knot in one of the ends.
Take a stitch at the edge of the leather to anchor the needle.
(Ex. 4.30) Then take one wrap clockwise around the dowel
and pick up two beads. This wrap is a base line to which the
first bead row is attached. **(Ex. 4.31)**

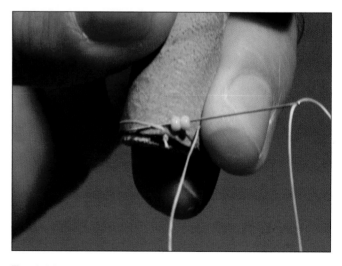

Ex. 4.29 Detail of brickwork.

Ex. 4.31

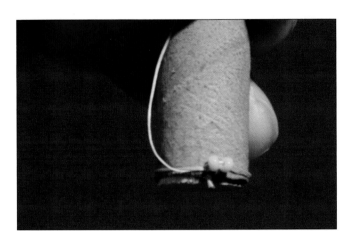

Ex. 4.32

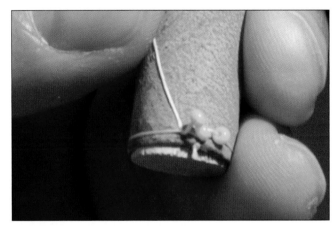

Ex. 4.34

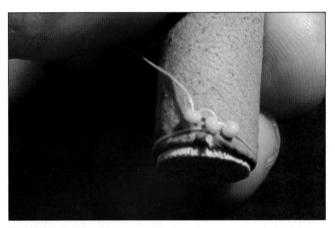

Ex. 4.35

Finish this wrap by taking a stitch behind and around the base line Put tension on the thread and snug the two beads up against the thread where it comes out of the leather. **(Ex. 4.32)** Now go into the left side and out the top of bead #2. **(Ex. 4.33)** Pick up bead #3, then stitch around the base line, first from the front of the base line thread then behind it. **(Ex. 4.34**) Complete this stitch by coming through the left end of bead #3 and out the top.   **(Ex. 4.35)** Now, pull the thread snug so that beads #2 and #3 touch. **(Ex. 4.36)**

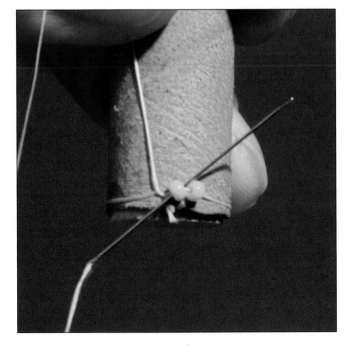

Ex. 4.33

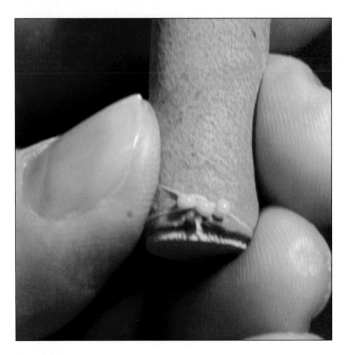

Ex. 4.36

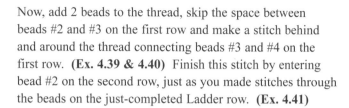

Continue to add beads in this manner until you reach bead #1, pulling the thread snug after each stitch. Before proceeding further, check to see how snug the circle of beads is. If it is a little loose, you should remove the last bead that you stitched on. Then, snug up the threads and see if the circle of beads is snug. It is better that this bead circle has a small gap between the last and first beads than be loose. If it is loose, all of the subsequent beadwork will not fit tightly against the dowel.

Once you have this Ladder row snug, note bead #1. Bead #1 will be laying more-or-less vertically. Enter the left side of bead #1 with the needle. **(Ex. 4.37)** Sew through the bead, then enter bead #2 from its bottom and exit from the top. **(Ex. 4.38)**

Now, add 2 beads to the thread, skip the space between beads #2 and #3 on the first row and make a stitch behind and around the thread connecting beads #3 and #4 on the first row. **(Ex. 4.39 & 4.40)** Finish this stitch by entering bead #2 on the second row, just as you made stitches through the beads on the just-completed Ladder row. **(Ex. 4.41)**

Ex. 4.39

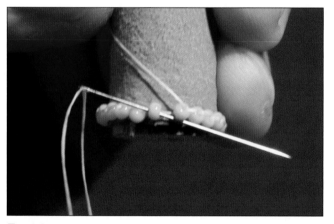

Ex. 4.37

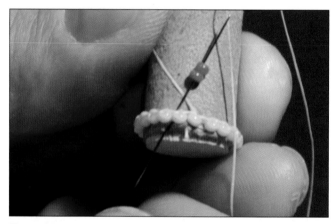

Ex. 4.40

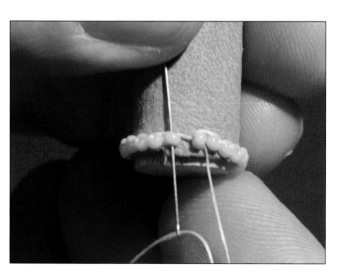

Ex. 4.38

Ex. 4.41

Continue by adding one bead at a time and stitching behind and around the threads on the first row. As you snug up the stitches, all of the beads will reposition and lay flat, like bricks.

At the completion of each row, go backwards (left to right) through the first bead **(Ex. 4.42)** and stitch through bead #2 from the bottom. **(Ex. 4.43)**

Adding Thread:

The best time to add thread is after you have completed a row by making the stitch just described through beads #1 and #2. See the illustration for the knot to tie with the old and new threads. **(Fig. 4 a thru d)**

1. Make a double loop near the end of the new thread. **4a**
2. Slip the loop over the tail of the old thread. **4b**
3. Pull the loop tight while sliding it down and as close as possible to bead #2. **4c**
4. Use the old thread to tie an overhand knot onto both strands of the new thread. **4d**
5. Trim the excess ends of both the old and new threads. You can leave 1/4" or so of each end, as you will hide this knot when you bead over it.

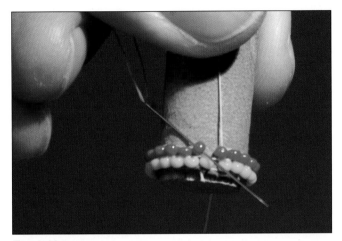

Ex. 4.42

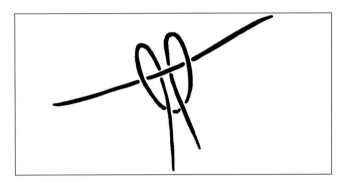

Fig. 4b

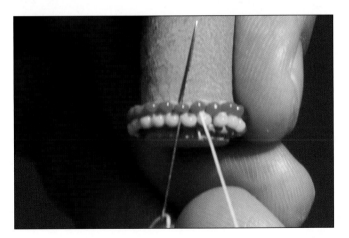

Ex. 4.43

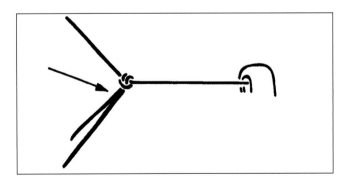

Fig. 4c

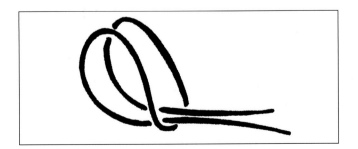

Fig. 4a

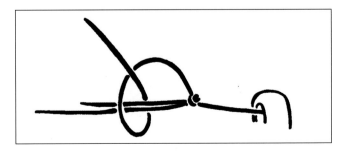

Fig. 4d

Creating Brickwork Designs:

As mentioned above, the design elements are the same as for 3-drop, and it does require a little planning ahead in order to incorporate the designs. Let's use a diamond as a design example and say that this little diamond will be 3 beads wide at the widest point. First, count the total number of beads that you already have in the first row, and let's say that it totals 20. With this number, we can have 4 diamonds with two background beads on each side of it. (Each diamond and one side of its background = 5 total beads).

If, however, we have 22 beads total width, we can still have 4 diamonds, only there will be 3 background beads between two of the diamonds. You might consider this okay, and, if so, you should put this design element on the back of the piece (a fan handle, for example) where it will be less noticeable. Another option would be to go back to the first row and take off two beads, thereby reducing the number to 21 total beads. It is always better to initially have a little space between the first and last bead of the first row, as this can then be maneuvered with your fingernail or an awl to remove the gap by putting a tiny bit more space between all of the beads. This will also allow you to pull your stitches tighter and the beads to bite into the material used to wrap the dowel.

Again, like 3-drop, design elements are often in odd number lots, such as 3, 5, 7, etc. It will be less frustrating to do a practice piece of brickwork before you actually begin a serious project. **(Ex. 4.44, 4.45, 4.46, & 4.47)**

Ex. 4.45

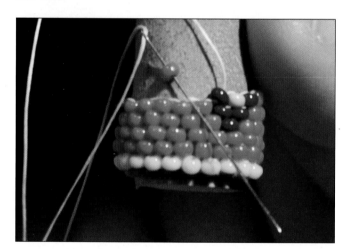

Ex. 4.46

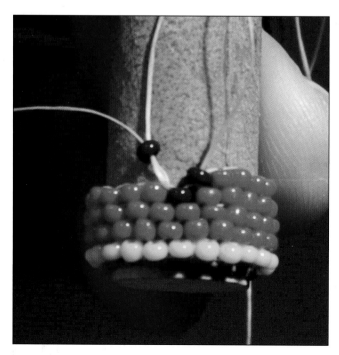

Ex. 4.44

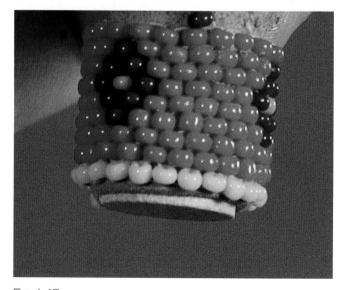

Ex. 4.47

Adding Beads:

Beads can be added at any place along a bead row to accommodate a widening shape. You can tell when it's time to add beads by the widening space between the first and last beads of a row. To add, attach two beads in two consecutive stitches to the same thread loop between beads on the row below. Again, choose two slender beads and try to make these additions in the background area. At first, this may take some trial-and-error as you learn to judge expansions, and you may have to undo a row you've done and redo it because you did not add the appropriate number of beads. Be patient, and you will improve your ability to judge as you bead along.

A-1 thru. 5: Peyote-beaded Fan Handles - by Scott Sutton

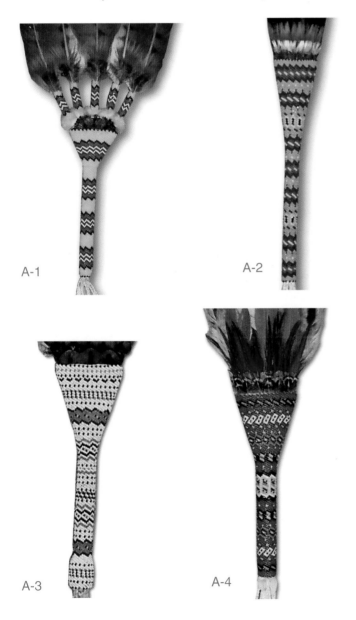

A-1   A-2

A-3   A-4

A-5

Loom-like Variation:

If you use the brickwork technique described so far, you will see that you will never have 2 or more beads lined up directly over each other to form a vertical straight line. There is a variation, however, that will allow you to do this, and the result looks like a section of loom work in the midst of brickwork technique.

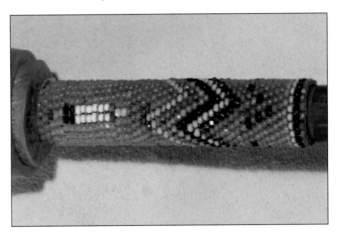

Ex. 4.48

Look closely at the straight vertical lines in the fan handle photo. **(Ex. 4.48)** Like loom work, all of the beads in the line are strung all at once on a single thread. For example, let's do vertical lines consisting of 5 beads. After you have finished a regular row of brickwork, string up 10 beads on the thread. **(Ex. 4.49)**

Ex. 4.49

Now make a stitch around the thread of the next row of beadwork below. **(Ex. 4.50)** Come up through the last 5 beads, then add 5 more beads. **(Ex. 4.51)** Make a stitch around the thread between the next brickwork stitch below, and, again, come back up through these 5 vertical beads. You can see that this technique is somewhat like edge-beading using 5 beads at a time.

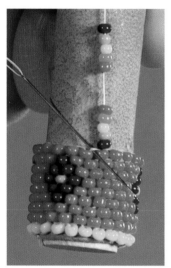
Ex. 4.50

Ex. 4.51

Continue making 5 bead stitches until you are back at the first vertical row. **(Ex. 4.52)** After stitching up through the last row, stitch down through the top of the first row. **(Ex. 4.53)** Anchor this first row by stitching around the connecting thread of the brickwork beads below and slightly to the right. **(Ex. 4.54)**

Ex. 4.52

Ex. 4.53

Ex. 4.54

Ex. 4.55

Now comes the "loom work" technique. Position the thread around the first bead in the first vertical row and wrap it from right to left around the entire first vertical row. **(Ex. 4.55)** End by stitching behind the thread positioned around the first bead. **(Ex. 4.56)** Move up to the next horizontal row and repeat this technique between the second and third beads of the vertical rows, then continue until you reach the top row.

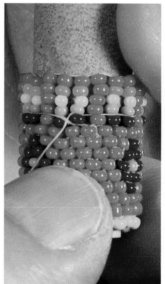
Ex. 4.56

Ex. 4.57

After wrapping around the fourth horizontal row, stitch behind the loop between the tops of the vertical rows **(Ex. 4.57)** Now it is a simple matter of resuming the brickwork technique.

Graph paper examples below shown in side views.

Peyote 3-Drop Graph Paper

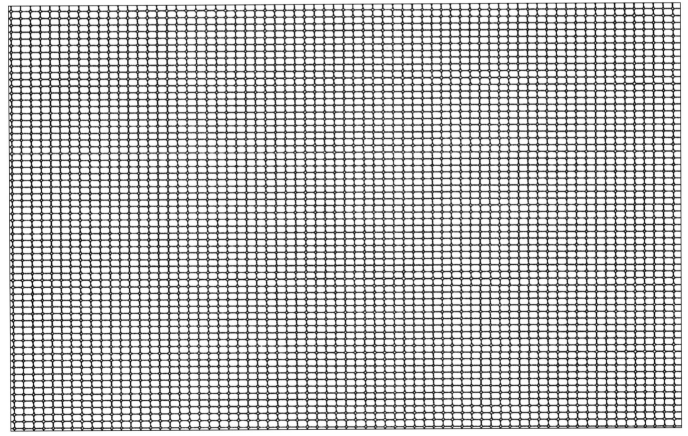

Loom Graph Paper

Gallery

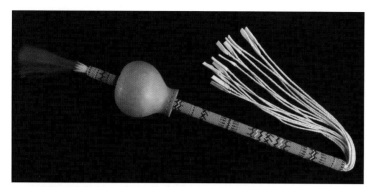

Gourd Rattle, by Steve Smith - Reddick Collection

Fan Handle, Brickwork by Joe Rush, Ponca - Reddick Collection

Loose Fan, Oklahoma - B. Hardin Collection

Peyote Gourd Rattles - B. Hardin Collection

Fan Handle, Oklahoma, Brickwork - Jerry Smith Collection

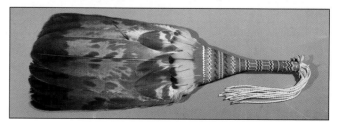

Flat Fan with Gourd Stitch Handle - Private Collection

Dance Stick, Kiowa/Comanche. B. Hardin Collection

Fans with Gourd stitch - Reddick Collection

Fan Handle Private Collection

Gourd Stitch Dance Stick - Jerry Smith Collection

Gourd Rattle in Brickwork Technique - Reddick Collection

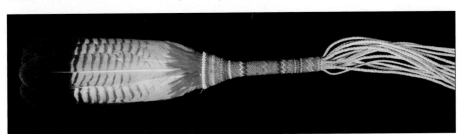

Flat Fan with Gourd Stitch Handle - Private Collection

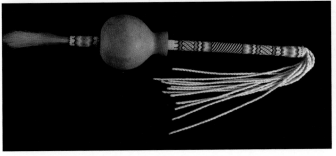

Gourd Rattle by Steve Smith - Reddick Collection

Flat Fan Handle
By Ben Stone

Sioux Cradle.
Reddick Collection

Lazy Stitch Beadwork 5

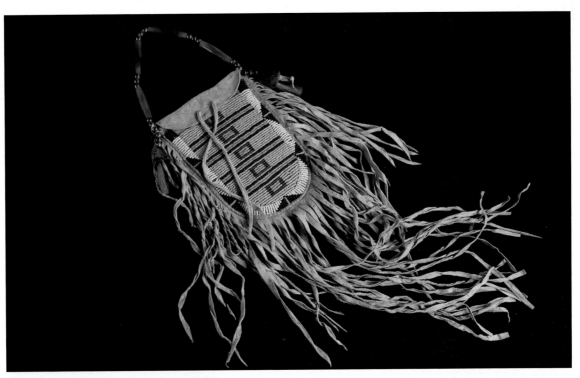

Sioux Beaded Bag Reproduction - CCTP

L azy stitch is one type of beadwork used to cover a large area. It is usually done on leather. Some of the popular dance items made using this style include moccasins, vests, aprons, armbands, pipe bags, dresses, and purses. Historically on the Northern Plains, almost anything made of leather was beaded in lazy stitch, including unusual items such as valises, pants, caps, etc.

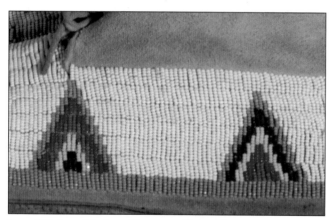

Materials:

Beads: Seed beads sizes 13/0, 12/0 and 11/0 are the most frequently used. Sometimes old bead colors are desired, and you may have to mix bead manufacturers. Make careful choices. Remember, beads from different countries are sized differently. Ideally, the beads you choose to use on a single project should be very close to being the same size.

Thread: Nymo size "D" works well. (Always double the thread.) Needles: 11 or 12 Sharps work the best; they are made for beading on hide. Beeswax: Applied frequently. Backing: There is no skimping on quality backing for this style of beadwork. Nothing can compare to brain tanned buckskin. Once you use it, you'll never bead on any other type of leather. Your needle will pass through brain tan like

Lazy Stitch on Modern Cheyenne Moccasins

butter! There are several books in print that give detailed instructions on how to brain tan hides. Although there is a great deal of physical work in tanning hides, it is not a complex process. If you have access to "green" (raw) hides, the economics may outweigh the intense labor. There is a commercially German tanned buckskin available that a beading needle passes through easily, and these hides are a close second choice. Other commercially tanned hides are not as desirable, as it is hard to get a needle through the hide. Native people always bead on the hide "the way the animal wore it," meaning, they bead on the hair side. If you don't want to bead on the smooth surface of a commercial hide, you must turn it over. Thus, you are beading on the "wrong" side, and it is harder to get the needle through commercially tanned hides. Avoid using split hides or suede hides. These hides have been broken down too much and will not hold up nearly as well. Miscellaneous: Sharp strong scissors, an awl (very sharp), a grid ruler, Glovers needles and sinew (real or synthetic) are other supplies that may be needed.

Layouts:

After you have chosen what project you are going to do, you will need to lay it out. Start by using bead graph paper to plot out a design. If a certain tribal style is being followed, careful research must be done to determine appropriate colors, design, scale of design, orientation of lanes, number of beads per lane, etc. Teepees, mountains, birds, pictographs and geometric shapes are design elements often used in lazy stitch beadwork.

When making garments such as shirts, pants, and coats from commercially tanned buckskins, it is a good idea to stretch the hides prior to layout and cutting. Begin by soaking the hide in warm water until thoroughly wet, then wring it out and squeeze as much water from it as possible. Important note: Do not try this with unsmoked brain-tanned hides, as it will ruin them.

Next, tack it to a large piece of plywood, a wall, or even a wooden fence. Start at the rear (tail) of the hide and stretch it from side to side and vertically, tacking around the rear legs. Move to the neck and pull it down and then out on each side, tacking according to the sequence of numbers shown. **(Fig. 1)** Finish stretching and tacking around the rest of the hide by always pulling out and away from the middle. Allow the hide to dry completely.

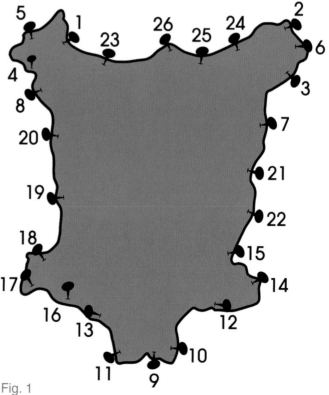

Fig. 1

The next step is to cut out the piece of hide. The piece needs to be laid out properly on the hide, depending on what is to be made. The bigger the project, the more important it is to lay it out correctly. For example, when doing a pair of moccasins, each one should be cut opposite the other on the hide. Use either the flanks or both sides of the back. This will assure you that both pieces will be of even thickness. A vest should be cut from the center of the hide, so that both sides will be even. Smaller projects may be cut from less important areas of a hide. It is wise to always lay out the project with the length going with the grain (the stretch) of the hide (i.e., oriented from head to tail on the hide). **(Ex. 5.01)**

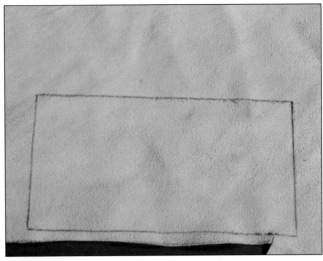

Ex. 5.02

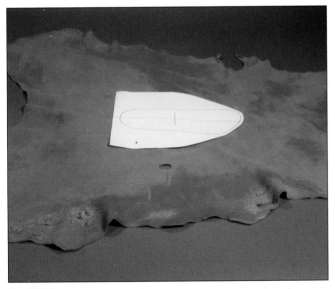

Ex. 5.01

Once the piece is cut out, draw a couple of lines on the side you plan to bead, the hair side of the hide. Since your design is already plotted on bead paper, a center vertical line and a horizontal line for the bottom edge of the first lane should suffice as guidelines. **(Ex. 5.03)** With a pencil, mark dark enough to see, but not so heavy as to cause smudge marks on the hide. DO NOT USE INK! Ink lines will be seen under the beadwork. Also, do not draw out the entire design because it will never fill in the way you think. Finally, draw only the bottom guideline or an occasional line to be sure your work is staying even. Do not draw out each lane. With a couple of guidelines drawn, it is time to start the beadwork.

It is a good idea to make a paper pattern (template) before cutting the hide. Good buckskin is not cheap; so, double-check the pattern position and measurements before taking out the scissors and cutting the hide. You do not get a second chance. As was mentioned earlier, the beadwork will be done on the hair side of the hide; therefore, the pattern should be laid out on the flesh side of the hide (the nappy side). Trace the pattern onto the hide while the hide is laying on a smooth flat surface. **(Ex. 5.02)** Do not stretch the hide and then cut, because you will be more than disappointed to find the piece shrink afterward. When tracing, use a pencil and not a pen. Try to cut just barely inside the pencil marks so they will not appear on the finished product.

Ex. 5.03

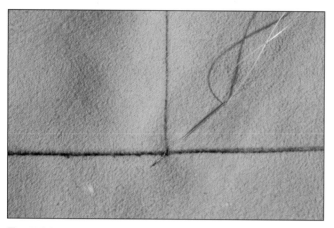

Technique:

Double thread an 11S or 12S needle with size "D" Nymo thread, and wax it moderately. Every few stitches thereafter, re-wax the thread. Knot the thread on the end with an over-hand knot. Clip the tail of the knot short. Long tails will stick up through the beadwork.

Your first bead row will be from the center of the design on the bottom lane. Start by piercing the hide in a place where the knot will be hidden by future bead rows. **(Ex. 5.04)** Do not go all the way through the hide. The point of the needle needs to come up through the hide at the intersection of your two guidelines.

as 5 beads per lane. It is much easier working off the hanks doing this style of beadwork, but you can use shallow containers if you prefer.

Following the design on the graph paper, pick up 8 beads in the desired colors with the needle and push them all the way down the thread. Lay the row down on the hide to determine the width of the lane. The lane width is the length of the 8 strung beads. **(Ex. 5.05)**

Ex. 5.04

Ex. 5.05

In lazy stitch beadwork, the size of beads is very important. Although the beads may have been purchased at the same time, different colors of the same designated size may be slightly different in actual size. Of particular importance is the background color in relationship to other colors. If the background beads are slightly thinner than the design beads, 9 beads may be needed for each row of solid background, while 8 beads per row are needed in the design area. It is okay for some rows to have more beads than the next as long as the width of the row is maintained. Having a different number of beads is preferred to having the lane vary in width. A series of shorter or longer rows may not affect the current lane, but, as you continue with other lanes, this will become a major issue. It is very important that the lane width be consistent.

Of course, as you go from project to project the lane widths may vary. Using 8 beads per lane seems to be a common number, even if you are working in very small beads. Some lanes on Kiowa moccasins/leggings may use as few

Lazy Stitch Beadwork on Sioux Cradle -
Reddick Collection

Ex. 5.06

Ex. 5.07

The stitch you make to attach the beads to the hide only goes part way into the hide, then out. **(Ex. 5.06)** It does not go completely through the hide and back up. **(Fig. 2)** The length of the stitch should be one bead wide. **(Fig. 3)** That will put the needle in position for the second row. It is important not to overshoot the length of the stitch, as this will create gaps between the rows. If you pull too tight to close the gap, it will cause the leather to shrink up, making the finished product too small. Conversely, if your stitch is too short, eventually the buckskin will start to roll up. In addition, the beadwork will not lay flat, and the beadwork will look bunched. Continue the lane by following the design using 8 beads to each row. Work your way out until you reach the rows of solid background color. Once the background rows are reached, bead for another couple of rows and stop. **(Ex. 5.07)**

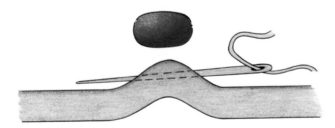

Fig. 2 Length of stitch equals one bead width.

Fig. 3

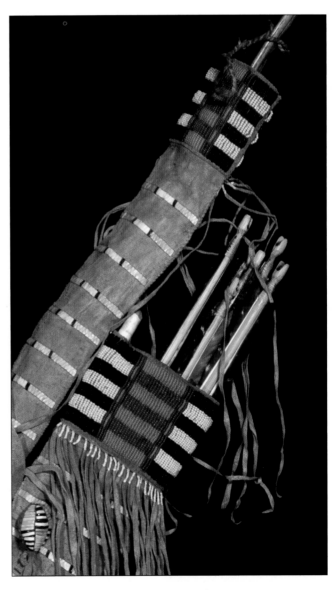

Lazy Stitch and Quill Work - Reddick Collection

Ex. 5.08

Tie off the thread by taking a couple of stitches into the hide that will eventually be covered up by subsequent bead rows. **(Ex. 5.08)** Knot the thread and clip the thread tail. Go back to the center and bead the other half (the right side) of the design until you are a couple of rows into the background. Tie off the thread. **(Ex. 5.09)**

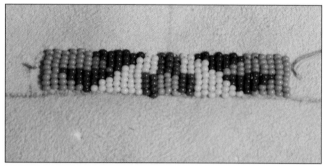

Ex. 5.09

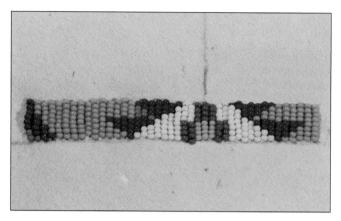

Ex. 5.10

To continue, move to the center of the next design on the same row you were just beading, then work back toward the first center design until the rows, in background color, meet. You may have to cheat on your row spacing just a "hair" to get the rows to meet exactly without crowding. **(Ex. 5.10)** Proceed in this manner until the bottom lane is complete, moving from the center of one design to meet the previously beaded section. Over the years, I have found it is best to complete the entire first lane before starting additional lanes. It seems that when several lanes are done one on top of the other before the completion of each lane, the hide can eventually shift, thus distorting the design. When one lane is finished, proceed to the next lane. **(Ex. 5.11)** Work either from the right or the left. The trick to the second lane is to interlock it with the previous lane.

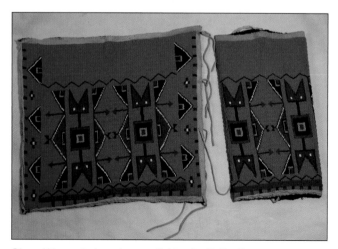

Sioux Woman's Leggings - B. Hardin Collection

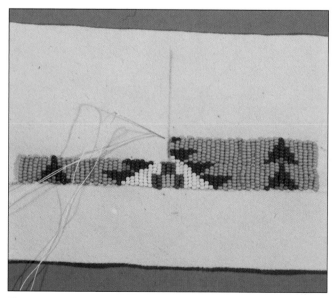

Ex. 5.11

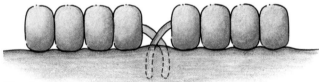

When the stitch is made to attach the first row of beads for lane #2, insert the needle into the leather just behind the previous stitch. **(Fig. 4)** All succeeding rows of lane #2 are done in this same manner. And so, lane #3 will interlock with lane #2, lane #4 with lane #3, and so on. The one thing that should be done differently is to bead each lane in the opposite direction. **(Ex. 5.12)** If you go right to left on row #2, then row #3 should be left to right. Sometimes, if you keep going the same direction, the beadwork will slant that way. Changing the direction as adjacent lanes are beaded will aid in keeping the rows straighter. The bigger the project, the harder it is to keep these rows straight. This is another reason why each lane should be completed before moving to the next lane.

Cheyenne Tobacco Bag Reproduction
Reddick Collection

Fig. 4

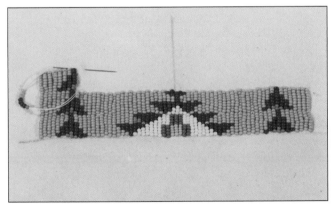

Ex. 5.12

Example of Lazy Stitch on a Pipebag

77

There are two choices in how the work will lay when it is done. It can either lay flat, **(Fig. 5 a & b)** or each lane can be slightly humped (rounded). **(Fig. 5c)** To make the work lay flat, continue beading as described above.
(Ex. 5.13) To make the lane humped, make the lane width smaller: one bead width short of flat. **(Ex. 5.14)** The same number of beads in a row in a shorter space will cause the row to rise up. This style will take constant measuring and very careful bead selection to assure that you are creating a uniform hump.

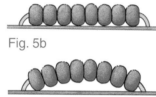

Fig. 5b

Fig. 5a   Fig. 5c

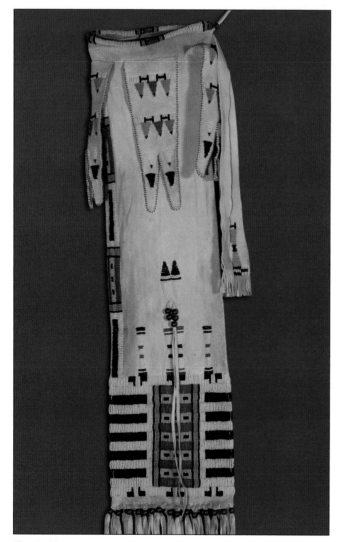

Ex. 5.13 Example of "flat" lazy stitch.

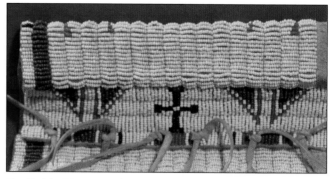

Ex. 5.14   Sioux Woman's Legging - Note Humped Bead Lanes - Reddick Collection

As you do your own research on those tribes that did major amounts of lazy stitch, you will find that, characteristically, Cheyenne work was flatter with interlocking stitches, while lanes of the Sioux were more rounded and not interlocked. **(Fig. 6)**

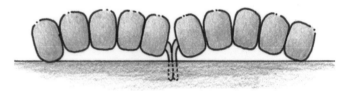

Fig. 6 Characteristic "humped" lanes

At this point, it is good to remember not to make the length of the stitch too long. Doing so will cause a reverse curling, and, if you force the work flat, there will be a great deal of stress on the threads, causing early deterioration of the beadwork.

Sioux Style Fully Beaded Dance Aprons and Side Tabs by Scott Sutton.

Gallery

Sioux Style Fully Beaded Vest by Scott Sutton.

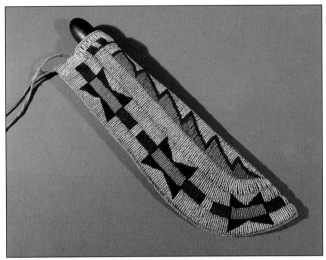

Cheyenne Style Knife Sheath - Reddick Collection

Sioux Style Vest by Scott Sutton - Back View.

Pipebag, Arapaho - Reddick Collection

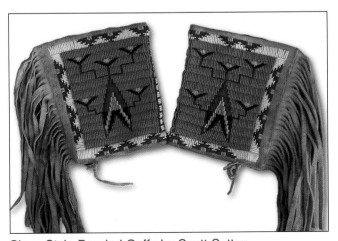

Sioux Style Beaded Cuffs by Scott Sutton.

Pipebag, Sioux Style Reproduction - B. Hardin Collection

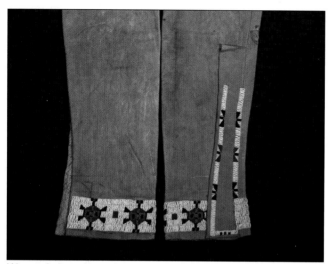

Woman's Leggings, Arapaho - Reddick Collection

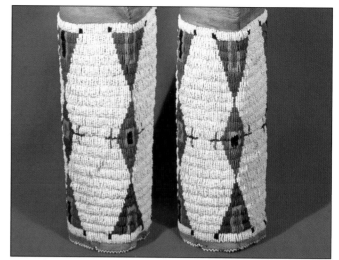

Woman's Leggings, Cheyenne - Reddick Collection

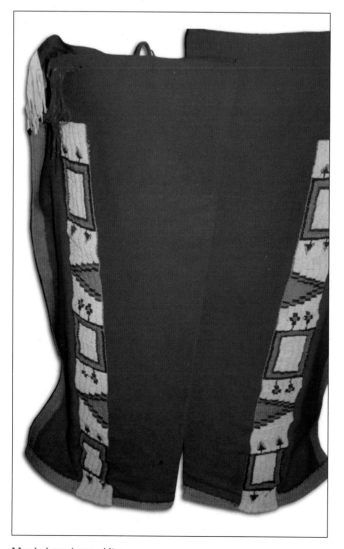

Man's Leggings - Ute

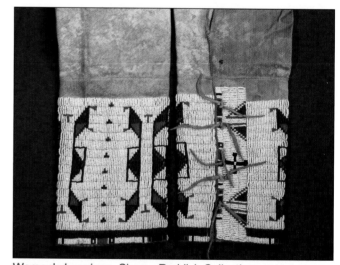

Woman's Leggings, Sioux - Reddick Collection

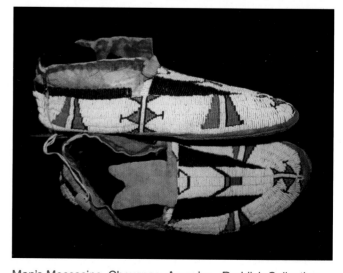

Man's Moccasins, Cheyenne, Arapaho - Reddick Collection

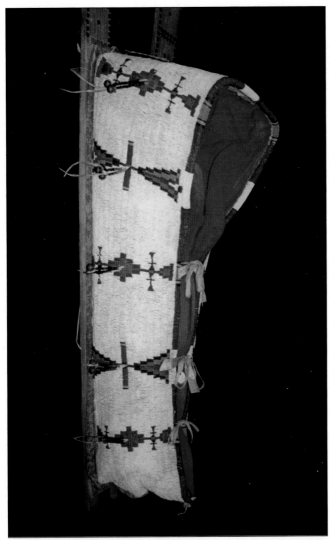

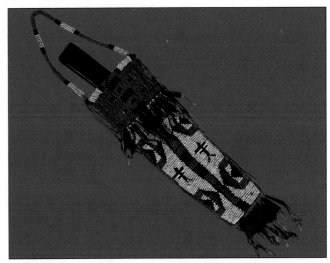

Knife Sheath, Cheyenne - Robert Wagner Collection

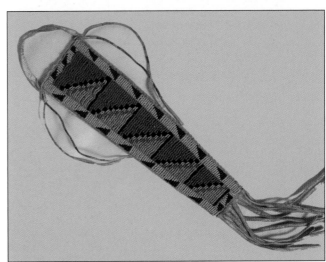

Knife Sheath, Sioux - Benson L. Lanford Collection

Cradle, Cheyenne - Reddick Collection

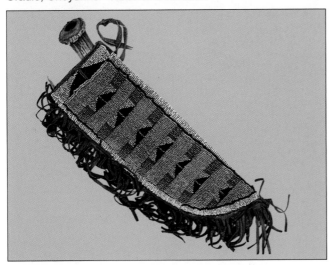

Knife Sheath, Crow - Heinz J. Bründl Collection

Moccasins, Northern Plains - B. Hardin Collection

Cheyenne - Reddick Collection

Plains Hard Soled Moccasins

Cheyenne - Reddick Collection

One of the most frequently beaded items using the lazy stitch technique is a pair of Plains hard soled moccasins. Making patterns to fit the foot is not easy. The following set of instructions will help you create a pattern for the sole and the upper so that you will have a pair of moccasins that truly fit. Sewing instructions are also included.

There is nothing that complements the look of a dance outfit more than a fine pair of beaded moccasins. Each tribe maintains its own unique styles and techniques of construction. But, currently throughout the powwow world, one style seems to be dominant: the two- piece hard sole moccasin. The buckskin part of the moccasin is called the upper, and, of course, the stiff latigo or rawhide bottom is called the sole. It is certainly possible for someone to take detailed measurements on moccasins stored in museums all around the country and then ascribe certain sole and upper characteristics to different tribes. But, you are only concerned with one question after dancing at a powwow for 4 hours: "Are my moccasins as comfortable as possible?" So, bottom line, make your moccasins fit your feet.

The following discussion tells how to make a generic Plains hard sole moccasin. The first step in making moccasins is to create a paper pattern for the uppers that fits your foot. **(Fig. 1)**

In order to make this pattern, you will need two measurements: first, the length of the foot and, second, the instep measurement, which is the distance from the ground across your arch and back to the ground. **(Fig. 2)** Using these two measurements, a pattern can be made that will fit with very little adjustment. Refer to the layout below and follow the directions to create a paper pattern.

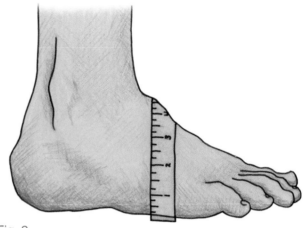

Fig. 2

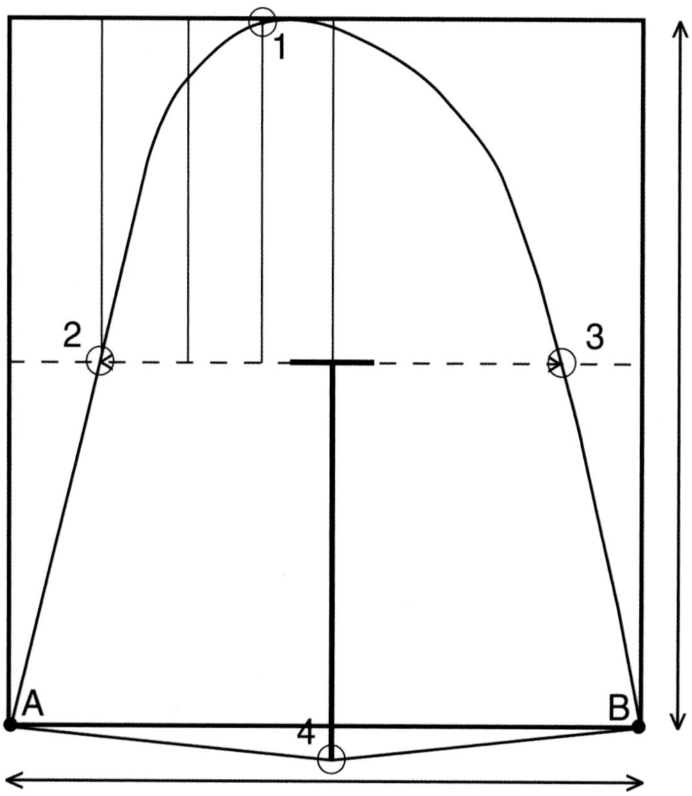

1. Construct a rectangle with the length being the length of the foot plus 1" for a foot that is 6-8" long or plus 1 ½" for a foot that is 9" or larger. The width of the rectangle will be the instep measurement plus 4 inches for the average foot. Add 1" for a wide foot and subtract 1" for a narrow foot.

2. Divide the rectangle into quarters.

3. In the upper left hand quadrant divide it into 4 equal parts vertically.

4. Put marks at Points 1 and 2.

5. Locate and mark Point 3, which is the distance of the instep measurement from Point 2 across the horizontal centerline.

6. Point 4 will be approximately ½" below the bottom center of the box.

7. These four points, along with the width of the rectangle (Points A to B), will form the landmarks to draw the perimeter of the upper.

Fig. 1

8. Draw the perimeter. From Point A (the bottom left hand corner), draw a straight line to Point 2, then continue that line and gently curve it over to Point 1.

9. From Point 1, arch the line to Point 3 (this portion of the curve will be an area that will allow adjustment if the foot is very wide or narrow) and continue from Point 3 to Point B (the bottom right corner of the box).

10. From points A and B at the bottom corners, draw two lines to Point 4. This will complete the upper perimeter.

11. Draw a "T" formation utilizing the vertical and horizontal centerlines. The top of the "T" is 1 ½" long. The leg of the "T" is drawn from Point 4 to the center of the "T" top. When you cut down this formation, it will create the opening for the foot.

12. Draw a second perimeter (not shown) ¼" larger than the first by starting at Point A, then proceeding clock-wise around the perimeter to B. This added area will be the portion turned under when sewing the upper to the sole. Place a mark on the edge of the pattern for Point 1. Note that this is the location for your big toe.

13. Cut the upper pattern out, including the "T". Place the paper pattern on your foot to see how well it fits. The pattern in the diagram is for the right foot. Turn it over and it becomes the left foot pattern. It should touch the ground with ¼" overhang all around. If fine adjustments need to be made, either trim off some paper or add paper using masking tape, then re-cut.

14. Once you have an upper pattern that fits, it is time to trace it onto the back of the buckskin for the upper. (Note: I always use brain-tanned hides, and these do not need to be pre-stretched. However, if you use commercial leather, it will need to be pre-stretched to avoid the finished moccasins stretching out of shape after they have been worn. See "layouts" section, p.72, **Fig.1**). Align the long axis of the pattern with the head-to-tail axis of the hide so that the pattern lays with the grain, meaning "with the stretch." If not, the result will be one moccasin which stretches and the other that does not. Trace the pattern, including the "T", and mark the leather at Point 1. Once you trace the pattern, be sure to turn it over before tracing again so that you will have both a right upper and a left upper.

15. Cut out the uppers but do not yet cut the "T" unless the moccasins are to be unbeaded. In that case, cut the "T" at this time.

16. Finally, make a pattern for the soles. **(Fig. 3)** Trace your foot with your sock off and keep the pencil perpendicular to the paper. Next, round off the tracing as indicated in the diagram. Some personal preference comes in here. Some people like the moccasin to fit very snugly, others prefer it to be a little loose. To make it tight, round the edges inside your foot tracing. To make it loose, round the edges on the outside of the tracing. On the sole pattern, note the location of your big toe and make a mark there. This will correspond with Point 1 on your upper pattern.

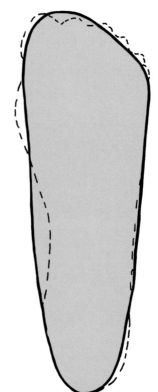

Fig. 3

Sioux - Jerry Smith Collection

Cheyenne woman's beaded mocs. The beading of fully beaded moccasin is discussed later in this chapter. However, we'll finish moccasin construction before addressing that. You should know that the moccasin upper needs to be beaded completely before you cut the "T". Once the beadwork is completed, cut the "T" and trim it off so that the length of the heel seam will be equal on both sides. See **Figure 4** for typical bead row layouts on the moccasins of The Cheyenne tribe.

Cheyenne Style Woman's Moccasins - by Scott Sutton

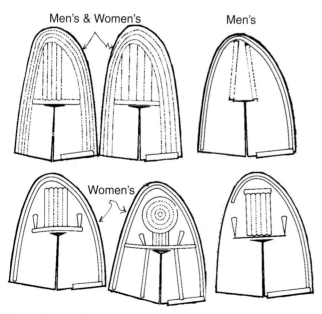

Fig. 4 Typical Cheyenne Beadwork Lane Placement

For the soles, use either latigo, a heavy, tanned strap leather, or real Indian-style rawhide for the soles. (There is a difference between Indian-style rawhide and the clear rawhide sold commercially. A good trading post will carry the correct material for soles.) I like to use white latigo for sole material.

When the upper is sewn to the sole, it is sewn inside out with the good side or beaded side touching the inside of the sole. When the sole has been attached, the moccasin is turned right side out, and then the heel seam is sewn. Of course, if there is to be a lane of beadwork covering the seam at the heel, it is beaded after stitching them together. **(Ex. 6.01)** Stitches should be about 1/8" apart and very tight. Either real sinew or imitation sinew should be used to sew the sole to the upper. An awl and Glover's needle also will be needed, as well as a good utility knife.

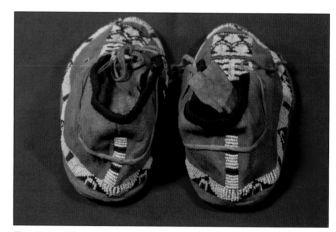

Ex. 6.01 Verticle lane of beadwork covering heel seam.

Start by cutting out the soles. (If using rawhide, it cuts easier if dampened. I actually soak my rawhide soles before trying to cut them.) I recommend Gingher scissors to cut with. Once the soles are cut out and dry, the following step will make it much easier to turn the finished moccasin inside-out: Bend the upper third (toe area) of the sole back and forth and side to side many times to limber it up. Don't stop until the front of the sole is quite flexible.

Before sewing the top to the sole, it is helpful to pierce a few holes with an awl in the edge of the soles along the toe area. Your awl should be a thin one whose point resembles a needle. The holes are pierced at an angle starting from about 1/8" in from the edge and on through the middle of the edge. **(Fig. 5)** Do not allow these holes to come out the bottom of the sole. Any stitches on the bottom of the sole will be worn out in one trip around the drum. Also, use a welt, as it helps extend the life of the moccasins and makes them more convenient to re-sole.

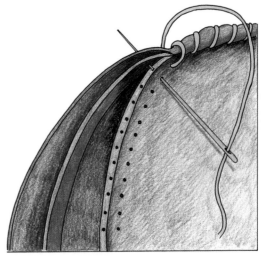

Fig. 5

A welt is a third piece of leather sandwiched between two pieces of leather while stitching them together. In this case, the welt is sewn between the sole and the upper. As the sole wears out, the upper is protected by the welt. Though the welt also may experience wear in some places, the fully beaded upper will remain undamaged. The idea is not to have to re-bead any section before re-soling the moccasins. For your welt, use the same buckskin that the moccasin upper is made from. Make it about ½" wide and about 2" longer than the sole perimeter.

Pierce these initial holes close together around the toe area back to the bump at the base of your big toe and approximately the same distance back on the outside of the toe. I also make my stitches closer together at the heel. These two areas need the most reinforcement from the stitching.

Place the sole over the moccasin upper so that the toe of the sole aligns with the toe of the upper. This is done by matching the marks for Point 1. **(Fig. 6)** To begin sewing the upper to the sole, start sewing by going through the pre-punched hole in the sole at Point 1 with a Glover's needle threaded with sinew (or imitation sinew). There is no knot, so leave about 8" of tail on the sinew. Hold the upper so that the welt is sandwiched between the upper and the sole, then stitch through all three pieces at this point. **(Fig. 7)** This will line up the moccasin upper on the sole correctly. Use a whip-stitch and make every stitch very tight, each time passing over the tail of the sinew. This will lock the sinew tail in place. Continue sewing either to the left or the right. If, after a few stitches, you feel it is necessary to tighten up these stitches even more by using an awl, be very careful. It is easy to inadvertently fray the sinew by splitting it.

Fig. 7   Stitching sole, welt and upper.

As you stitch around the sole edge, do not pull or stretch the upper. In fact, the top may even need some little puckers ever so slightly as you go around the toe. It is a good idea to check and see that the top of the "T" remains perpendicular to the centerline of the sole as you sew along. Also check alignment by frequently placing the upper around the sole to make sure that it is going to make the entire distance to the center of the heel.

Whip stitch the upper to the sole until you reach the center of the heel curve, Point B, and remember to make your stitches very tight and closer together as you approach the heel. If you have done a superb job of measuring and sewing, Point B hits exactly in the center of the heel. If there is a small excess of upper buckskin, it can be trimmed off. If Point B is short of the center of the heel, you will have to take out some stitching and try again.

When you reach the center of the heel again, hopefully Point A meets there also, or you may have to do some trimming as before. After you have completed sewing the upper to the heel's center, reverse direction and continue making additional stitches back toward the toe for about 1 1/2"-2" on each side. This will result in a doubly reinforced heel area. Use the same holes, if possible, but just be careful to not cut any of the first stitches when you go back through the holes. These back stitches will end the thread, and so there is no need for a knot or underweaving.

Once the sole is attached, turn the moccasin right side out. Starting at the heel, flip the inside to the outside. Continue on up to the toe area. The area around the instep is the toughest and may be very frustrating. In this section, keep working side to side in very small increments, and eventually you will reach a point where the rest will turn easily. I sometimes use a blunted round dowel to help me turn these and then smooth out the seam.

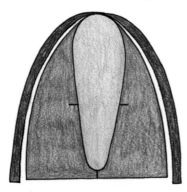

Fig. 6   Match centers of sole, welt and moccasin top.

Once turned, sew up the heel seam using a baseball stitch. **(Fig. 8)** This will make a flat seam which is desirable if you are going to bead over this seam. At this point, you should trim the welt. Use a good sharp pair of scissors to trim any excess away until you have a uniform width of welt showing. Cut as close to the upper and to the sole edge as possible, but be careful not to cut any stitches. Cutting stitches should be almost impossible if the stitches are very tight.

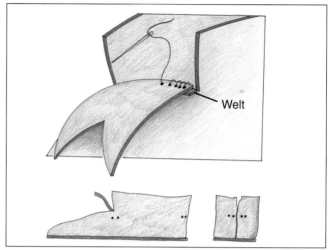

Fig. 10

Ties can be visible or covered with the top lane of beadwork. **(Ex. 6.02)** If the uppers are not fully beaded, punch holes to accommodate the ties in the upper and thread them in to place. Make the ties from the same buckskin as the uppers. They should tie on the top of the instep like any other shoe. **(Ex. 6.03)** If the uppers are fully beaded, quite often the moccasin tie is behind the lane of lazy stitch beadwork that occupies the position where the ties would normally go if they were partially beaded. This lane serves as a tunnel for the tie. The tie can be seen at the heel seam where it travels over (more like in between) the bead rows of the heel seam as these rows run parallel with the moccasin tie.

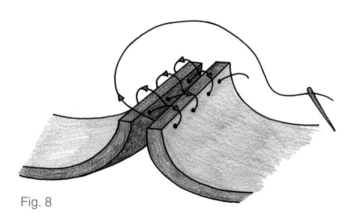

Fig. 8

To finish the moccasins, add tongues and ties. **(Fig. 9)** Tongues come in a variety of shapes and sizes. Make them wide enough to span the top part of the "T" cut. Tongues of fully beaded moccasins may or may not be fully beaded. They are sewn to the upper using a whipstitch and incorporating a welt. **(Fig. 10)**

Ex. 6.02
Cheyenne -
Jerry Smith Collection

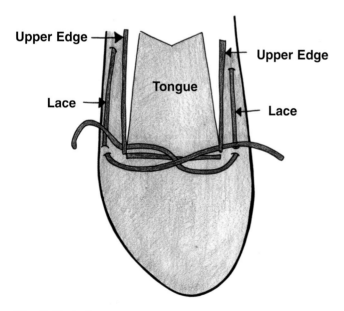

Fig. 9 Typical placement of ties on Cheyenne moccasions.

Ex. 6.03

Cheyenne - Jerry Smith Collection

Beading Moccasins

While a great deal of this chapter is devoted to the construction of the "Plains Hard Soled Moccasins", this book is on beadwork, so a little time needs to be devoted to some tricks I've used over the years. Having beaded well over 100 pairs, I've learned several techniques that may be helpful to you in completing a set of moccasins that fit and look great.

Of the "Plains Hard Soled Moccasin", there are basically two types: partially beaded and fully beaded. These styles use the Lazy Stitch technique. Other types of moccasins employ Appliqué technique, either directly on the upper or as a separate piece that is sewn on later. But the vast majority of beaded moccasins today are done using lazy stitch. The pattern in this chapter is used for both these styles.

Some concern needs to be given to the material of which these moccasins will be constructed. In the chapter on Lazy Stitch, it was mentioned that the manner in which the pattern is laid out on the hide is important. This is so that the stretch for both moccasins will go the same direction. Also, the hide itself must be taken into consideration: Too thin and it will stretch too much. Too thick and it will be hard to work with. If you select a hide that is medium weight and has little stretch either way, then you will not have to alter your pattern. If you are doing a partially beaded pair and the hide is stretchy, you may have difficulty in keeping them in the correct shape. If possible, pre-stretch the hide so that there is not so much give to it. If that is not possible, be aware that, as the moccasins are worn, they will stretch.

In addition, there are many other styles of moccasins, including high tops, one piece, soft soles, and boots, just to name a few. To go into detail on all these is well beyond the scope of this one chapter. So, let's concentrate on the two styles that the pattern included in the chapter will help you construct: the Plains Hard Soled Fully and Partially Beaded Moccasins.

Fully Beaded

When doing a pair of fully beaded moccasins, some research needs to be done to find design elements that will be appropriate for a tribal origin you may be following. In addition to the design, research will help you in the selection of colors and style of beads for the project, particularly if you are doing a period piece. One of the most popular styles of Plains Hard Soled Moccasins is of Cheyenne origin. The vast majority of moccasins that I have made are of this type.

In selecting beads, buy enough to finish the entire project and have enough left over for repairs in the future should you break beads due to rough dancing or wear and tear. Several sizes can be used in a project like this. Common selections include 11/0, 12/0 or 13/0 Czech beads. For the extra special pair, "cut" beads (Charlottes), either 13/0 or 11/0, may be used. My personal favorites are the 11/0 "cuts".

Cheyenne - Reddick Collection

Although colors vary a great deal (and in the powwow world you will see many different colors of background), traditionally, white was the predominant background color. Sometimes light blue was used. Today, I've seen orange, green, red, black, and yellow, just to name a few as background colors. The greatest concern in choosing colors is to make sure they contrast with each other. For example, if you choose to make the background light blue, you would not want to use a medium blue to start a design next to the light blue. It would not be a good contrast. However, choosing a dark blue or red would be striking next to the light blue. With your design in hand, choose colors that will go well together as a whole and will contrast next to each other. Think "light to dark and back to light again". Try to avoid a cascade of shades, such as light blue, medium blue, periwinkle, and dark blue. These colors will all blur together and not be very striking against each other.

Other supplies you will need include Sharp needles (size 11 or 12 work best), pure beeswax, size "D" thread (always doubled), or sinew (not recommended for beginners). A pair of sharp scissors, an awl (very sharp, often you need to grind the point yourself) and flat pliers come in handy while doing the beadwork.

Using the pattern in this chapter, the beadwork will start ¼ inch from the edge. Remember, the tops should be beaded before the moccasin is constructed. Make sure you are on the correct side of the leather. If using brain tanned buckskin, you need to be on the hair side of the hide. Usually this is the smoother side of the hide. The nappy side of the hide is the wrong side. If using commercial hide, you need to bead on the nappy side. Just be aware that it will be harder to get the needle through the hide.

Typically, Cheyenne moccasins have seven perimeter designs, one on the toe and three down each side. For a very small foot, five patterns may be used. Conversely, for a very large foot, nine patterns may be used. As just mentioned, one design is on the toe, and it should be placed so that it will hit between the great toe and the second toe. Don't place it over the pointiest part of the pattern. Make a small mark on the upper at what will be the center of the toe design. Remember, the bead lane will be ¼ inch from the edge. If we are using seven patterns, we will have three down each side. The middle of these should be placed where the "T" cut of the upper is placed. The one on either side of that is spaced evenly along the edge. The placement of the designs should be done on the instep side of the foot first. After those marks have been placed, do the outside of the foot. **(Ex. 6.04)** Both of these heel designs should be in approximately the same place. The front design of the outside of the foot might need to be placed a little further forward so that, when the design is beaded, the top of it will end across from the front design on the instep side. You should now be looking at an upper that has the "T" marked (for cutting later) and seven marks which will be the centers of each design element for the perimeter of the moccasin.

Sioux Style Moccasins - Don Drefke Collection

Let's Bead!

It is time to start beading. I do not mark a perimeter guideline here, but it may help with the first couple of pairs you do. If you do mark a guideline for the perimeter, use pencil and do it as light as possible. This line will be ¼ inch from the edge of the upper. Do not include the back of the upper. The best way to fully bead moccasins is to start in the center of the toe of the perimeter and work your way out to the background as described in the "Lazy Stitch" chapter. Note: Here is one of the great tricks of doing moccasins: Ease the stitches around the toe. That means always keep them at a 90 degree angle to the center of the upper. The result is that the stitch between bead rows on the outside edge of the first lane will be slightly wider than the inside edge of the first lane. **(Ex. 6.05)**

Ex. 6.04   Cheyenne Style by B. Hardin

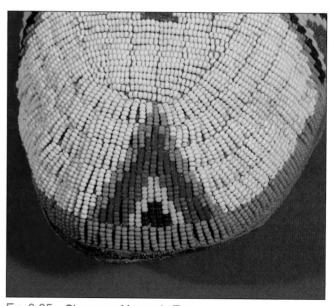
Ex. 6.05   Cheyenne Moccasin Toe

With your Sharp needle threaded, folded over double and waxed, enter the hide from the approximate center of what will be the first lane and come out on the center dot you have marked on the toe. Your needle is now in correct position to start your work. It is important to remember that, if you want the work to lay flat, then make the lane only as wide as your beads will allow. For example, if you are using 8 beads to a row, string them on the needle and slide them down to the end of the thread. Then lay them on the upper at a 90 degree angle to the starting point, aiming towards the center of the upper. Make the stitch to secure the first bead row. If you want a raised look (more common among the Lakota people), follow the same process but make the stitch 1 bead width narrower. This will cause the bead lane to hump up. Continue to bead this center design out to the point where the background starts, plus one or two more rows. Tie off the thread as described in the "Lazy Stitch" Chapter.

Next, go to the first side design closest to where you ended the center background. Start in the center of this design and bead back towards the toe. When you get to the background of this side design, continue to ease the lane around the curve until you hit the background lanes where you ended coming from the toe. Tie off the thread as before. Go back and finish the other half of the toe design until you get to the background, plus one or two more rows. Repeat this process on the other side of the moccasin. Continue this way until all seven designs are complete. When you bead from the center of the back design towards what will be the heel seam, stop ¼ inch from the edge. As you tie the thread off, make sure the knot is under the lane of beads just completed, not in the heel seam area. Looking down at the upper, you should have the first lane of beadwork completed around the entire perimeter of the upper. **(Fig. 11)**

It is time to anchor the thread for the second row, the idea being to interlock this thread with the center row of the first lane you beaded. Starting along the center line of the toe, stitch into the hide in the bare area of the second lane and come out under and behind the center row of the first lane. Your needle and thread are now in position to start beading. String the beads according to your pattern and line them up 90 degrees to the toe. Then make your stitch the same as above. Again, you are going to ease your stitches around the corner.

Don't try to line up each stitch of the second row with the rows of the first lane. You can only do this when you start a new row so that the lanes stack up on each other. Trying to interlock lanes will end in disastrous results. This is because I usually find that, as I bead a lane, I need to make the upper stitch a little narrower and the bottom stitch a little wider as I make the bottom stitches of this row behind the upper stitches of the lower lane. When doing this, the wider stitch is about 1½ rows wide. (This is just an approximation.) Work it so that the rows are 90 degrees. When you look at these rows, you will see gaps at the bottom and sometime slight cramping at the top. This is to be expected. **(Ex. 6.06)**

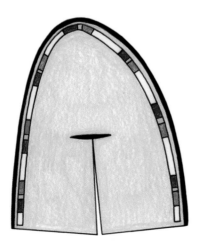

Fig. 11 Example of Cheyenne Uppers.

Ex. 6.06 Detail view showing typical bead lane placement at the toe.

Continue to work your way around the moccasin to the back. You don't have to start in the center of each of the side designs anymore, but you must keep the side designs lined up so that your pattern matches with the lane below it. Once you go around one side, start back in the center of the toe and do the other side. Row two is completed.

Depending on your design, you may have two, three or four rows around the perimeter. Rarely, five rows are done, but, if you do five, it is very difficult to "turn" the toe design on this row. So be prepared for a struggle. Note: Regardless of how many rows you do, as you do each row, it gets harder to turn the toe and make it look good. It will take some patience and work to get those stitches just right to make them even and smooth. When three lanes are used, it is fairly easy to make all the turns. The fourth row starts to get more difficult. This also depends a great deal on the size of the upper you are making. A women's small foot will make it much harder to turn the third row than a man's large foot.

Once the perimeter is finished, proceed to bead the instep row (if there is one). This is that single row across the instep just under the "T" where the tongue will attach. **(Fig. 4)** Center any design at the center of the "T". When this is complete you will have the top and the cuffs left to finish.

The starting point for beading the top is dependent on the design you have chosen. If the design is an odd number of lanes wide, you start half a row from center at the instep row and bead towards the toe. If the design is an even number of lanes, you start in the center of the instep row and bead towards the toe. Work your way to the outsides of the toe area. Once the design is finished, continue until you have filled in all your background.

Sioux - B. Hardin Collection

Some bead-workers like to also bead the cuffs. This is not required but really puts a nice finished touch to the moccasin. If you decide to bead the cuffs, continue beading up from and parallel to the previous lanes. Often on Cheyenne moccasin there is a solid row of a different color beaded to set the cuff apart from the perimeter. This is not a requirement but again is a nice touch. If I am going to bead the cuff, I put the lace under the first row of the cuff. So the lace should be cut and put in the upper as describe earlier. Care must be taken not to catch the lace in the bead stitch. The cuff section is usually 3 rows consisting of the solid one and then 2 with design in them.

Once all the beadwork is completed, it is time to cut the "T" and put the moccasin together as described earlier in this chapter.

After the upper is sewn to the sole, the heel seam needs to be beaded. Again this is done using the Lazy Stitch technique. This consists of a vertical bead lane the same width as each perimeter lane and starts even with the bottom perimeter row. It extends up as far as the cuffs are beaded. The perimeter rows should touch the heel seam row. If they do not, then complete beading them at this time.

The tongues may or may not be beaded and should be sewn into place at this time. If the laces were not put under the row of beadwork, they should be placed now to complete the project.

Cheyenne - Reddick Collection

Partially Beaded:

Partially beaded moccasins are done very similarly to fully beaded ones. However, there are some distinct differences. First of all, since they are not going to be fully beaded, keeping the lanes straight and the rows tight is even more important. Bead the first perimeter lane just like you did for the fully beaded example. Keep all your knots under this one lane. Subsequent lanes may come down the toe area, across the instep, or cover the laces. Regardless of where these lanes are placed, you must keep your lanes straight. Use a very light pencil line to assure one edge of each lane is straight. Often, the heel seam of partially beaded moccasins is beaded all the way up.

Cheyenne - B. Hardin Collection

Cheyenne Child's Moccasin tops - B. Hardin Collection

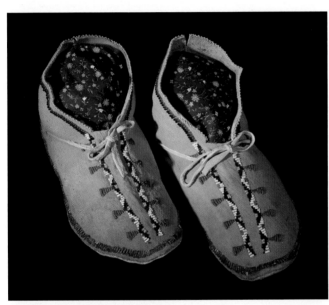

Apache - Don Drefke Collection

Summary

Now that you have read this book cover to cover, you are well on your way to becoming a great beadworker. Many books spend a great deal of time on designs, but I feel it is much more important to get the "how to do it" part down. Designs are easy. To master the techniques is to develop an art form.

Following the guidelines given in this book will give you the necessary building blocks to master these four beadwork techniques. Mastering them will allow you to create many beadwork projects that will have that fine look of art to them. Be patient with yourself. It is very humbling to remember some of the first pieces I did. It gives me a chuckle when I think back on them. I never had a guide such as this book that really told me all the nuts and bolts of doing beadwork. If I had, I would have saved myself hundreds of frustrating hours. Now you have the benefit of how to perform these techniques without having to undergo all my trials and errors, and so you can skip some of the frustrating parts and go right to the "I can do this!" stage.

Continued practice in these techniques will assure your continued growth as a bead-worker. This is a beautiful art form, and, as any artist will tell you, you must continue to apply yourself if you are going to be any good at it. Now is your time. Happy beading!

Prairie - Don Drefke Collection

Gallery

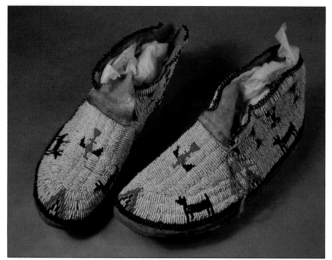

Cheyenne - Jerry Smith Collection

Arapaho - Reddick Collection

Cheyenne Woman's Moccasins - Reddick Collection

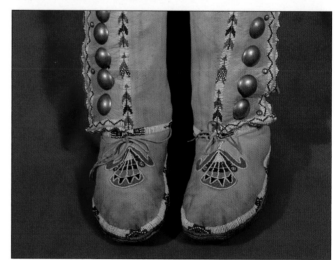

Kiowa Woman's Boots - Reddick Collection

Sioux Moccasins - Reddick Collection

Cheyenne/Arapaho - Reddick Collection

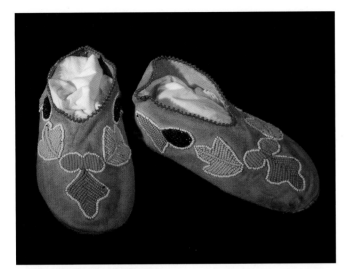

Prairie - D. Drefke Collection

Prairie - D. Drefke Collection

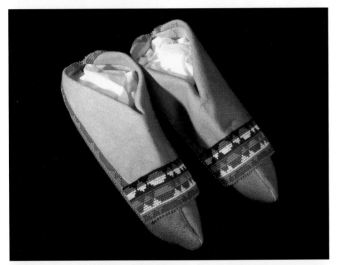

Winnebago - D. Drefke Collection

Kiowa Women's Leggings -
Reddick Collection

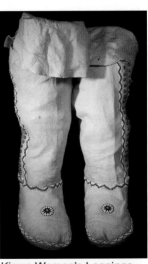

Kiowa Women's Leggings -
Private Collection

Southern Cheyenne Man's Moccasins - Keven Hiebert Collection

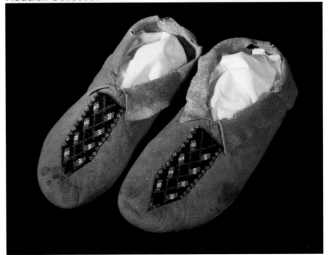

Kickapoo - D. Drefke Collection

Meet the Author:

When I was a youth of 5, my Father and I joined Y-Indian Guides. Shortly after joining, my Dad bought me a bead loom and the book *Indian Crafts and Lore* by Ben Hunt from Tandy Leather Company. I beaded my first loom piece when I was 6 years old and, thus, started a life long passion.

Later, through the Boy Scouts of America, I joined the Tribe of Tahquitz, the honor scouting program for Long Beach, California. That program had a strong Native American influence. Shortly after joining, I went to my first powwow and was hooked!

I struggled with beadwork, but through this organization and the California Indian Hobbyist Association (CIHA), I met some great teachers like Jerry Smith and Corrine Fry. I began beading almost anything and everything!

By the time I was 17, I was spending a great deal of time going to powwows (singing and dancing), researching in museums, and, of course, DOING BEADWORK! Spending the time at powwows and museums helped me to develop some of the techniques I am sharing in this book. But, I must tell you that God must get a great deal of the credit. He gave me an incredible gift to create and design out of my head without having to draw things out. And, with His additional gift of the use of my hands and eyes, I have been blessed with the ability to do most craft work by just looking at it and then doing it.

My favorite beadwork technique is appliqué. It is very versatile and may be used in so many different ways. Next, I like lazy stitch. I get a kick out of going to a dance and looking around at how many dancers are wearing moccasins I have beaded! However, it is wise to master all four techniques in order to be an accomplished beadworker.
As the years have passed, I've attended powwows all over the country. I've enjoyed Fancy Dancing, Straight Dancing, Traditional Dancing and Singing (both Northern and Southern). Besides Hethushka Dancing (formal War Dancing), I mostly attend Native American powwows with my local community in Oregon. My wife and I are members of the White Wolf Singers, of which I am the lead singer and teacher. My passion, however, is beadwork!

Scott Sutton wearing his Straight Dance outfit.